THE BIBLE

TEXT BY CLAUS WESTERMANN

PHOTOGRAPHY BY ERICH LESSING

THE BIBLE

A PICTORIAL HISTORY

A CROSSROAD BOOK

THE SEABURY PRESS · NEW YORK

1977
The Seabury Press
815 Second Avenue
New York, N.Y. 10017

Original edition: "Le message de l'espérance",
© Hatier Éditions S.A. Fribourg 1976.
This edition copyright:
© Verlag Herder GmbH & Co. KG, Freiburg im Breisgau 1976.
Library of Congress Catalog Card Number: 78-8383
ISBN: 0-8164-1216-2
Printed in France by Imprimerie Gaston Maillet, St-Ouen (illustrations)
and in West Germany by Freiburger Graphische Betriebe (text).

CONTENTS

THE BOOK

A thousand years went into the making of the Old Testament. It was not written as a single study, but grew like a tree, a crystal, or a great mountain-range. It encompasses the history of a people; and the voices that testify to this history are many and varied. The reader of the Old Testament has to be aware of these voices because much of this book was first expressed in the spoken word. Most of it grew out of the actual life of the people of Israel; and long passages had often been repeated and transmitted orally for centuries before being committed to writing at a later stage of tradition. This book can really only be known by entering into the living process of creation and development that the words went through; and by trying to understand the individuals who uttered them and the society in which they were once spoken. The words were an essential part of the life of the people.

Israel's book contains songs which expressed moments of overpowering joy, and then became fixed in the minds of the people, without changing over hundreds of years. There are also stories which were obviously told and re-told, acquiring many new details and emphases in the re-telling. There are commandments and laws which passed without change into written collections after long years of oral tradition. There are political documents and accounts of highly personal experiences; there are records of entire historical periods, liturgies for divine service, priestly instruction, and a vast prophetic literature. There are even love-songs and laments for the dead in this astonishing book.

All these diverse oral and written traditions are bound together by a single consistent and dominant theme: a great dialogue with which the book is concerned from beginning to end. This is a continual exchange between God and his people, between God and the world, and between God and the individual; this is the special mark of the book which we call the Old Testament. A single dramatic action extends from the first page to the last. From the start, the men the book tells us about find themselves in a position of confrontation. They are challenged by the living God – their origin and their goal. They are his creatures, and the goal which their life aims at can only be his work. This basic relationship or tension between man and his creator includes and surpasses all possible and conceivable tensions between ordinary earthly events, thus giving a powerful and living unity, a perpetual current, to each individual action and detail.

The best way to gain an overall picture of the various writings which make up the Old

Testament is to start with the divisions that were gradually made as they were handed on – the headings under which they were first grasped as a whole. The three main parts are: the historical, the prophetic, and the didactic books.

The first basic form is that of narrative, under which heading come the Torah (the Pentateuch or the five books of Moses), the historical books from Joshua to 2 Kings, the work of the Chronicler, and the Book of Esther.

The second basic element is God's speaking to man. This is found above all in the prophetic books, which contain the words of God addressed to his people through his messengers, the prophets.

A third basic element is man's speaking to God. This is found above all in the Psalms, but is not confined to them. There are many other examples. "Wisdom" may be considered a forth basic element, found chiefly but not exclusively in the Book of Proverbs.

The first three elements on which the division of the biblical canon is based are essentially connected. The Old Testament is the story of an event set in motion by what God said to Israel; Israel's answer in praise and lamentation is part of this event. Even these basic elements display the dialogue characteristic of all the events of the Bible. The Bible is not so much a book which makes statements about God, or "teaches us something" about him, as one which tells of a series of events launched by a word spoken into history. The book speaks of a people and individuals caught up in a single event impelled by two forces: the word – and the answer given.

"Wisdom" is the only element of the Old Testament which does not seem to fit into this scheme. But it has an essential part to play in it. The Old Testament is not concerned only with dramatic happenings. The action does not take place merely in God's deeds and men's deeds, in words and answers, in obedience and disobedience. There is always another, very different factor, a calm activity of God which the Bible calls "blessing". The counterpart of this is "wisdom", which grows out of the ripeness of experience in answer to the work of the creator; therefore wisdom is no mere marginal phenomenon for the people of God.

Of course these three or perhaps four basic elements are not found only in the Old Testament. The Swiss scholar Emil Staiger defines the three basic elements of Western literature as the epic, the lyrical, and the dramatic, and claims that these are fundamental aspects not only of literature but of the whole of human life. Despite the different contexts and subject-matter of the literature examined by Staiger, the epic has a parallel in the historical writing of the Old Testament, lyrical poetry in the laments and hymns of the Psalter, and the dramatic in the drama between God and his people which is played out in the prophecy of Israel. In both cases the basic theme of the drama is sin and punishment. Staiger also offers the didactic poem as a fourth possible element; this could be compared to the wisdom of the Old Testament.

In the Old Testament these basic elements produce action of an astonishing range: from the universal to the particular, from the immensity of the cosmos to the detailed conversation of a father and son on the road; from the glory of the stars to a single human being's cry of anguish.

The creation of the world begins the Old Testament narratives, and its end is spoken of in the apocalyptic texts of the latest period. The whole action of the Old Testament is a unity. Everything that happens is seen in the light of a beginning that points to a certain end, no matter what is involved – a human life, the life of a people, the nations of the earth, humanity itself, or even the whole universe. The Bible thinks in terms of the whole, and so, in the first eleven chapters of the Book of Genesis, it begins with a "story of the origins" in which everything that exists – the world and man, coming to be and passing away, death and calamity, progress in culture and the blessing of growth – is referred back to its origin: creation and the creator. Although most of the Book is the story of one small nation, insignificant from the point of view of world history, the story is set from beginning to end in the framework of universal history – the history of man and the universe as outlined in the "story of the origins".

In the Bible, the course of the stars in the heavens and a child's laughter, the development of nations in history and a domestic quarrel which ends in peace, are equally important. The book's immense range and its message of God, of his words and his deeds, are two aspects of the same reality.

The Bible also joins other extremes; it bridges, for example, the gulf between the holy and the profane. Although the Bible is a sacred book read and explained at divine service, the language used in it is often very simple, close to ordinary life, and far from solemn. The most ancient documents of the Old Testament (and of the New) were composed in a simple, vivid and direct language still remote from the solemn and sacred, from the abstract and theological. The language of the first three gospels of the New Testament and that of the oldest part of the Pentateuch (the so-called "Yahwist" document) are remarkably simple and concrete, and devoid of special sacred and theological expressions. Yet the later documents of both Testaments use a firmly theological or sacred terminology – most evident in the Pentateuch in the "Priestly" writings, its most recent section. Both sacred and the profane ways of speaking have their own place and time and therefore their justification; hence both appear in the Old Testament. Their use also means that human talk about God can take many forms and has a history of its own. It can change in the course of time, for God cannot, so to speak, be restricted to any type of language.

Of course, throughout centuries of translation and re-translation, the Bible has been put into many languages. People who know Hebrew, the language of the Old Testament, are constantly amazed that sayings, stories, commandments and acclamations have passed from

Hebrew into Aramaic, Greek and Latin, then into the modern European languages, and finally into nearly all the tongues of the modern world, and yet have kept the meaning they had for their hearers.

Naturally, all translation has its limits. "Thou shalt not kill", the fifth commandment, has a very different ring in the original. Nevertheless the transmission of the Bible through many languages, and eventually into present-day languages, brings a reality from the world of the past into the living present. When we hear the *De Profundis* (Psalm 130) or the psalm which speaks of the short life of man and the everlasting life of God (Psalm 90) recited at a grave-side, we are linked with the people to whom these words were first addressed. The language of the Bible has an importance of its own, since it is so rich in human possibilities, experience and wisdom. The language of the Old Testament has many special qualities which made it the right sort of language to carry the events recorded in it through thousands of years. Scholars still find such characteristics a rich field of study. It is significant that, after being a language dead for many hundreds of years, and known only to a few people in any form, the language of the Old Testament has been revived in the modern State of Israel. At Tel-Aviv airport you will hear the same greeting that met the pilgrim as he entered the gate of Jerusalem in the time of David.

The Old Testament is sacred Scripture for the Christian church as well as for the Jewish synagogue. It is the national and the historical book of the modern State of Israel; it is also highly esteemed in Islam. It can reconcile strong contrasts, and its significance as a unifying factor will one day be manifest.

THE PEOPLE AND THEIR HISTORY

MEETING

The story related in the Bible begins with a meeting that took place when a small group of men were in great distress. As they combined with many other groups and clans, this small tribal group grew into the people of Israel. They were suffering oppression in Egypt; as an even smaller group they had left an impoverished region or had been driven by famine to take refuge in Egypt, where they found bread and work. But as they multiplied they were exploited through forced labour. Their longing for freedom was answered by a great event, which launched the history of the people of Israel and gave it an indelible stamp. Their liberation was not merely the first step in the history of Israel, but the key-note of their relationship to God for ever after. The basic shared experience was that of the depths of misery. A new era began with the experience of deliverance.

This drama was not confined to some special religious sphere but took place in the clear light of day. In the midst of harsh realities the Israelites encountered a saviour God. The meeting took place in real life. One of the Israelites, whom tradition calls Moses, brought a message to these victims of forced labour: "The God of your fathers has sent me. He will free you." The group had to decide to believe this message and trust the messenger – who was wholly without credentials. They made an act of faith, followed him, and began the history of Israel. This first experience of deliverance was to leave its mark on them for ever. A word announcing freedom hat reached them, and they had relied on this word. A messenger had appeared; they had trusted and followed him. They had met the God of freedom. Now, as they set out on their way, they knew they would always be under the guidance of a God whom they knew, and who had come to them as the saviour God.

Their trust was soon put to a severe test. With the Egyptians in pursuit, they found themselves in grave danger.

When the danger grew acute immediately after the Exodus, the promise made by this God became a reality. When distress seemed greatest, by the Red Sea, the Israelites were saved from danger, and we still have a song – probably the oldest in the Old Testament – in which they sang the praises of the saviour God:

Sing to the Lord,
for he has triumphed gloriously;
the horse and his rider he has thrown into the sea.

These events represent the fundamental experience of Israel with its God – a very human experience. To go through the successive stages of distress, rescue and joyful thanksgiving can be part of human life at all times and in all places. The experience itself is nothing very special. What is unique is that in this case the single experience of deliverance from suffering forged a bond between the suppliants and the saviour God; this bond began and coloured a history that has lasted until the present day.

This one experience of God gave a lasting insight: God is he who saves from the depths. Seen from the standpoint of this first hour, more than half a millennium of the history of Israel is illuminated: in a similar situation, after the destruction of the State and the temple in the Babylonian exile, the people's relationship to God remains basically the same. Events have the same rhythm: distress and a cry for help, longing for deliverance, salvation from God and a hymn of praise from the rescued. But one thing has changed. In the intervening period, guilt – the great sins of the people against God who once delivered them – has accumulated. The new intervention, rescue from the Babylonian exile, can be based only on forgiveness, which is almost the mainspring of God's new saving act. Now Israel acclaims freedom with the cry:

Comfort, comfort my people, says your God.
Speak tenderly to Jerusalem, and cry to her
that her time of service is ended, that her iniquity is pardoned.

Christians also believe that, five hundred years later, God was again announced as the saviour of Israel; but deliverance was separated from the history of the national State to become a forgiveness extended to all humanity through a saviour – God become man. For Christians, the message of the Israelite Jesus is the message of freedom, given as part of that same history that grew out of the original meeting with God.

The praise and thanks with which the people greeted their rescuer did not last; for they were delivered not into a paradise but into the desert. The group that had been rescued from Egypt had to endure the dangers and trials of a journey that meant hunger and thirst, exhaustion and despair. We read that the people rebelled against God on their journey and complained against their leader. But, surprisingly, the story of the desert wanderings simply records complaints and revolt as something comparable to the severity of the trials; for the protection of God was not relaxed: rescue came again and again with each new threat. They had the new experience of God the protector and guide, who remains true to his people even

12

when they rebel at the harsh experiences of the way through the desert. This put a new and lasting element into the dialogue. The saviour God is not there just in the one glorious hour of deliverance; he stays. He is always with his people in the dangers and temptations of the way, even when his own, embittered and accusing, turn against him. This is what this group of men called out by God learned on the way; and the experience, in one form or another, from then on was part of the history of the people of God.

During the desert years, another meeting took place between God and his people; it was different from anything that had been spoken of before. The scene of this encounter, the "mountain of God" in the desert, is called Sinai or Horeb. It cannot be identified with certainty. But the pictures of the mountains of the Sinai desert give us a faithful impression of the mountain beneath which the Isrealites rested. It had been a holy mountain for hundreds or thousands of years before the Israelites reached its foot. In the new experience of revelation at Mount Sinai, the history of Israel is like that of the many religions in which a holy place, and especially a holy mountain, have decisive importance. The story of the revelation on Sinai deals with a monumental event, but presents it with extreme reserve and through allusions. The top of the mountain, covered with clouds, is screened off, and this separation makes it a holy place. But for Israel the only significance of the holiness of this place is that the holy God speaks from it.

The Sinai narrative has restraint yet immense power. A voice from the clouds on the mountain tells Moses to come. The radiant of God, to the accompaniment of thunder and lightning, descends on the mountain top, which is still hidden by its mantle of cloud from the eyes of the people. The people wait at the foot, for they are forbidden to walk on the mountain. At the appointed hour Moses ascends the mountain, alone. The people do not see the meeting, which is of a very special kind, quite different from the encounter with the saviour. It is the sacred event, of the kind fundamental to all divine worship of later times: the apparition of God in the sacred place, represented by his glory descending on the mountain top; the entry of the priest into the holy of holies, represented by Moses' climb to the hidden summit.

This two-way movement – God descending and the mediator ascending to the holy place – has as its goal the utterance of God's word; but it is not the same as the divine words spoken in a historical situation in order to change events. It is the special word spoken in the holy place: in the stillness of sacred time. In priestly tradition, the divine word from the holy mountain is an order to construct the "tent of meeting", the shrine carried from place to place by the people as they wander through the desert, and a model of the sanctuary to be built later at Jerusalem. In this way, the early history of the people, at the centre of which is the God who saves and guides, is joined with later times, when they have settled down and the temple has become the centre of national life.

In the older traditions, God's commandments were revealed on Mount Sinai. These commandments were fundamentally important for all subsequent history. Direction by commandments is now added to the particular directives for the way. "Torah" – direction, instruction – came to stand for all the commandments and laws defined on the basis of those first simple commandments, and collected in the various codes. Commandments and laws indicated a way of serving God: the answer of praise was now accompanied by the answer of service. But whenever the people refused to respond with service, disregarding the commandments and the will of God audible in them, his judgment had to take its course. The commandments given on Sinai indicated the course of prophecy: the announcement of judgment.

The interchange described above is summed up in the Old Testament by the term "covenant". Only in Israel was this term, essentially a political one and used to cover a wide range of treaties, alliances, pacts and contracts, applied to the relationship between the people and God. It brings out the unconditional nature of the obligations arising from the encounter between them. It is a mutual relationship in which the free promise of the people to serve and obey only this God corresponds to God's promise to be the God of this people. The solemn ratification of the covenant between God and Israel was also linked with the holy mountain in the desert. The unique event that took place there became a lasting part of the covenant – the swearing of loyalty on both sides.

The first breach of the covenant was the first major event after the departure from Sinai. The worship of the golden calf violated the order not to make images of God. The breach of the covenant was followed by God's intervention. But the mediator, by his intercession, saved the people from the worst judgment; and the mercy of God enabled them to continue their journey.

Therefore the first stage of Israel's history, from the exodus from Egypt to the eve of the entry into the promised land, contains in germ all the essential elements of Israel's later history, the further acts of the drama played out between God and his people. Only when we recognize these pointers can we see that this history, despite the major differences which characterize and contrast each phase, is still consistent.

PRE-HISTORY

THE PATRIARCHS   When Moses announced the day of freedom to the oppressed tribes in Egypt, he told them that his message came from the God of their fathers. This links the story which begins with the rescue from Egypt with the stories of the patriarchs in the second section of the Book of Genesis (chs. 12–50). The stories of the patriarchs are a precious record of an early age. The kernel of the stories certainly stems from oral tradition. And the origins of this patriarchal tradition (as has been proved only recently) are to be sought in a period which precedes by centuries the process of fixing them in writing and of linking them with the history of the people. They originated centuries before the exodus from Egypt. Here archaeological research has made a very important contribution to the elucidation of a section of the Bible. Not so many years ago most Old Testament scholars were convinced that the stories of the patriarchs were largely composed by the writers who inserted them into their great works of national history; but recent archaeology has shown that a large number of the place-names and personal names, customs, practices and laws can be assigned to the first part of the second millennium, and were to be found in the very territories with which tradition associated the wanderings of the patriarchs.

This places the story of the patriarchs in a new, broad perspective. We now know that their origin and growth, from the first oral narratives, extends over many hundreds of years. And this long growth of the patriarchal traditions can be traced in considerable detail. Only in the final stage of their composition, when they were inserted among the major passages linking them with the history of the people, did they take on the form in which large spans of time were greatly compressed, and which now gives the impression that they deal only with the three generations immediately before the migration of the children of Jacob into Egypt to escape a famine – the three generations of Abraham, Isaac and Jacob. In reality, whole epochs are reflected in the stories of the patriarchs.

If we read the stories of the patriarchs one after another, we can see the theme of the promise running through them all. A promise had inspired trust in the little group in Egypt when it set out to make its way through the desert. It was the promise of the land, which made the wanderings of this early period into a consistent whole – an epoch in history. The promise became one of the basic themes of the history of Israel down to the New Testament, which saw Christ as the fulfilment of the whole chain of promise. By using the same theme, the great history-writers of the time of the monarchy succeeded in linking the history of the patriarchs to the history of the people; for the land where the Israelites finally found a home had already been promised to the fathers when they were wandering in it as strangers.

The story of Abram, to whom God later gave the name of Abraham, begins with a promise:

> The Lord said to Abram,
> "Go from your country,
> and your kindred and your father's house
> to the land that I will show you.
> And I will make of you a great nation,

and I will bless you and make your name great,
so that you will be a blessing.
I will bless those that bless you,
and him who curses you I will curse;
and in you all the families of the earth will be blessed."
(Genesis 12:1–3)

With this promise the narrator joins together one of the ancestors of the people from the obscure past, which represents an epoch long before the beginning of national history, and the Israel of his own day. The promise reaches out far beyond the narrator's time to take in an unknown future where the blessing of Abraham is to be felt. Hence this great span of blessing is a firm bond joining the time of the patriarchs with the history of the people.

This promise of blessing, of the land, of a son, of descendants, runs through the whole history of the patriarchs. It is linked with a theophany, as in the verses immediately following. It is the climax of a narrative, as in the next chapter. It gives rise to special stories of promises, as in chapters 15 and 17; and it occurs in several combinations of themes and additions, as for instance in Genesis 22:15–18. The promise is also a leitmotif in the stories of Isaac and Jacob, where it is mostly referred back to the promise to Abraham.

This texture of promises is itself an interpretation of the ancient narratives, and gives the stories of the patriarchs an orientation to the future. The hearer of the narratives feels that he himself is treading the way along which the fathers travelled in the distant past towards the promised blessing, land, and future.

In this way the author or authors succeeded in doing something achieved so successfully nowhere else in world history. The unifying theme of the promise preserved in tradition a stage of the pre-history of the people which elsewhere either disappeared entirely, or could only survive in fragments. The stories of the patriarchs preserve something essential from the period before the settlement of the people in the land. At that early stage the ancestors of the Israelites were semi-nomads, travelling to and fro with herds of sheep and goats, tilling the soil at the same time – or between their travels, as occasion offered. They lived and moved in small groups. The special features which distinguished their existence from the life of the people of Israel have been faithfully preserved in the stories of the patriarchs. These semi-nomads did not form a state; the clan and the family were the only common framework in their lives. Almost nothing of a political nature occurs in the stories. There are no wars. Nothing is said of Abraham, Isaac or Jacob being citizens of any state. Any kings who occur in the narrative are strangers. All the usual features of national history are absent. The only exception is the 14th chapter of Genesis, which tells of Abraham giving battle to four kings. But this chapter is foreign to the ordinary presentation of the age of the patriarchs; it represents another perspective, which transfers Abraham into the sphere of political events. The contrast with chapter 14 makes it all the clearer that the rest of the story of the patriarchs reveals a way of life in which the members of the community had not yet developed a political form of existence.

What we are told about Abraham, Isaac, Jacob and Joseph remains within the sphere of family life. It is the history of a family – the reflection of a form of life which is of great significance for the history of mankind, even though it has mostly disappeared entirely from the traditions of the advanced cultures.

The family life, which is today only a sector of "life", once embraced the whole sphere of existence. Nothing mattered but the family – its relationships, adventures, preservation or destruction. All the social and political processes which appear later in the various forms of human society are contained here in essence. Life may become at times more dramatic, tragic and intense, but it all remains within the sphere of the family. The stories of the patriarchs must be read in this perspective.

The patriarchal history is built up round three generations, each of which reflects a basic preoccupation of family life. In the history of Abraham, Genesis 12–25, everything turns on the birth of the child. The existence and survival of the family depend on a son being born. In the history of Jacob and Esau, Genesis 25–36, the theme is the co-existence of two brothers – the sibling relationship. In the story of Joseph, Genesis 37–50, the theme is how the attitude of the father to one son differs from his attitude to the others. This reflects the transition from family life to forms of society which have branched out more widely. The very fact that the three sets of themes are divided up and assigned one by one to the three parts of the history of the patriarchs shows that the sequence of the three generations from Abraham to the sons of Jacob is not meant just to represent the mere succession of three generations. It is a picture of the familial form of life in its most important manifestations.

Another closely connected characteristic of the stories of the patriarchs is that they describe an existence which is pre-cultic just as it is pre-political. This means that divine worship, in the later form such as is known from the history of the people of Israel, did not yet exist. Some basic elements of later worship may already be noted: the invocation of God, or prayer, sacrifice, the sacred place, the altar. But there is nothing of the permanent institution about them, and, above all, the cultic office of mediator is missing. The father himself offers sacrifice. This direct approach to divine worship goes hand in hand with the direct approach to God. The opening words of the history of the patriarchs, as quoted above, are typical of this immediate relationship with God. God spoke to Abraham, we are told, as if it were something quite natural. This immediacy is characteristic of all that takes place between God and man in the stories of the fathers. Here we have a distant echo of the conviction that the gulf between the present world and God, the necessity of a human mediator and of an institution mediating between God and man, are things that strictly speaking are out of place in the relationship between God and man.

This direct relationship to God marks all the stories of the patriarchs and gives them a beauty of their own which corresponds to the simplicity of the relations between men as well as between God and men. Everything in the stories is so human that it can still speak directly from the distant past to men of every age. The special relationship to God in which he comes so close to man and in which there is no need of any mediating factors finds expression in the titles of God in these stories. He is the "God of the fathers", the God of Abraham, Isaac and Jacob, the "Mighty One of Jacob", and so on. The narrators distinguish clearly between God as he was known to the people since saving them from the bondage of Egypt, and the God of patriarchal times. The narrators recognized that this concept of God belonged to another epoch. The distinction between the God of the fathers and the God of the people of Israel indicated in the different names has been confirmed by recent study of comparative religion. Research into the religious environment of the ancestors of Israel has helped to define more clearly the historical differences between the two conceptions.

The stories of the patriarchs cannot be discussed in detail here. They still speak so vigorously after thousands of years that men of all degrees of culture can hear something in them that links them with their own lives. They deal with the elemental processes of human life: birth and death, a mother rejoicing and a mother despairing, quarrels and reconciliation, love and hatred, fellowship foundering and fellowship restored, hail and farewell, laughter and tears, hunger and thirst, comfort and forgiveness.

Two terms in particular characterize the events in the story of the patriarchs: "blessing" and "peace". Essentially, blessing means the power of fecundity, of growth, of success. The power of the blessing makes it possible for generation to succeed generation in the course of history. The same force passes on the life of the parents in the birth and growth of the son. Through the power of the blessing a woman is honoured in the community as the mother of her children. The Hebrew word for peace, *shalom*, really means the well-being of a community. It is the well-being of the community that is at stake in the quarrel between Jacob and Esau. The story of Joseph begins with a break-down in the soundness of family life, and it ends with the family fellowship being restored. This peace ist not really something that men can bring about. Peace here means rather the life-giving element implanted in a small community, without which human fellowship cannot exist. Just as God is the author of blessing, so he gives and safeguards peace.

THE BEGINNING OF TIME The story told in the Old Testament does not begin with the patriarchs, but with the creation of the world and of man. Nevertheless, a distinction is made between the national history which begins with the exodus from Egypt, the pre-history which tells the story of the people's ancestors, and an event which is at the basis not only of the history of Israel but of the history of the world and of mankind – the story of the origins. This takes in more than the creation of the world and of man. The first eleven chapters of Genesis deal with a history which comprises creation and the flood, the expulsion of man from paradise, various stories of crime and punishment, and the story of the dispersal of mankind. It is held together by a series of genealogies that link the history of origins with the history of the patriarchs, and extend from the creation of man to the beginning of the narratives about Abraham.

The universal background of the first eleven chapters of Genesis has important bearing on all that is narrated in the Bible. God's covenant with *one* people and bringing of redemption through *one* saviour, related in the middle of the Bible, comes within a universal history which links the beginning of the world and of mankind with the end. This universal character is the great *obbligato* which can be heard softly or strongly on every page of the Bible.

Creation narratives were not confined to the great advanced cultures of Asia, Europe and America. Primitive peoples in many parts of the earth had their creation stories, in a great variety of forms. For many thousands of years the creation of the world and mankind was basic to all thinking about the world and mankind. Nevertheless, the advanced cultures, in Egypt in particular, were mainly concerned with depicting the creation of the universe, whereas the majority of creation stories in primitive cultures deal with the creation of man. A possible deduction is that the question of the creation of man arose earlier in human history than that of the creation of the world.

The creation stories of the Bible combine the two elements. In the later presentation of creation in Genesis 1:1 – 2:4a, the real theme is the creation of the world, while in the earlier, Genesis 2:4b – 3:24, it is the creation of man. There is a special reason for the inexhaustible depth of these stories. The two pictures of creation come at the end of a long tradition. To understand them one must start from the fact that a large number of creation traditions, narratives and motifs have been worked into them. This is the only way in which they gain significance for present-day readers. They make accessible to us an explanation of the world and mankind which dominated the thinking of mankind for thousands of years, and without which even our current scientific explanation of the origin of the world and mankind is not comprehensible.

We are near the end of the period in which the scientific explanation of the origin of the world and of mankind could be played off against the biblical discourse about creator and creation. Continued study of the first chapters of the Bible has made it increasingly obvious that to say that the world was created by God does not preclude a scientific explanation of the first ages of the world and mankind. The creation narratives in the Bible were not intended to describe exactly *how* the world was made and *how* man came into existence. This is shown by the fact that the descriptions of how creation took place can vary from text to text in Genesis 1–3, and in other parts of the Old Testament which deal with creation. The Old Testament allows various ideas about creation. It can say that the creator is like an artist who moulds or constructs something out of his materials. It can also say that God produces everything by a word. We are not entitled to reject either of these concepts for the other. The different approaches to the idea of creation in the Bible bring out the real point of the story, which is to assert that man's mind and imagination can never penetrate the mystery of creation. All that the Bible has to say about the making of the world is meant to inspire reverence and praise for the creator, a theme which occurs again und again in the Psalms:

> Let all the earth fear the Lord,
> let all the inhabitants of the world stand in awe of him!
> For he spoke, and it came to be;
> he commanded, and it stood forth.
> (Psalm 33:8–9)

But the theme of the first chapters of the Bible is not confined to creation. Genesis 1–11 is a self-contained composition in which each unit has something essential to say about the history of the origins. The creation of the world and mankind is balanced by the story of the flood (Genesis 6–9). Since the world is God's creation and man is God's creature, the existence of the world and the life of men are in God's hands. The creator can wipe out his work. The recognition of God as the creator implies the possibility of this extreme measure. And this means that existence is never taken for granted. Hence the narrative of the great catastrophe which overwhelmed the whole earth is an intrinsic part of the story of the beginnings. This powerful story, which shows the human race almost totally destroyed by the flood, is there to affirm impressively to each new generation that mankind can only be preserved from destruction by the hand of the creator. The flood is closely linked to the great theme of preservation: the world must be upheld; it does not simply function as a matter of course. In the face of all possible and imaginable disasters, this theme of preservation points to the power which can save from the abyss. The creation narrative can be properly understood only together with the story of the flood. The creator retains the power to dispose of his work absolutely as he wills: to destroy it or to preserve it. But by preserving his work, he remains present to each generation.

The story of the flood at the beginning of the Bible has yet another meaning. When the waters have flowed away, God makes the promise: "While the earth remains, seedtime and harvest, cold and heat, summer and winter, day and night, shall not cease" (Genesis 8:22). These words, "While the earth remains", point from afar to an end which will come one day. In the Bible, the beginning of time has the end of time as its counterpart. Catastrophe comes upon the world at the end as at the outset. The fact that creation remains at the disposition of the creator also means that he will one day bring the course of the world to an end. The story of the origins conjures up the story of the end – the apocalyptic vision.

The truth of man's being a creature is not the whole story of his coming from the hand of God. It is also an essential element of man's existence that he is finite, limited. This means that the story of man's creation (Genesis 2) is closely linked with the story of his failure and of his estrangement from God (Genesis 3). These two chapters are among the finest things ever written about human nature. Nothing that man himself can achieve, no honour that one man can pay to another, can compare with the dignity which he has as God's creature. But a recognition of his dignity inevitably goes hand in hand with an acknowledgement of his limitations. He must return to the earth from which he was taken. Being a man, he can go wrong and offend. But man, despite his limitations, is entrusted by his creator with the world and the future, and this is his dignity (see Psalm 8).

Episode after episode in the story of the origins brings man's great limitation more and more clearly to light: he constantly tries to be something more than himself. He tries to be "like God". He disobeys God's command, because a higher degree of life seems to him more important than this command (Genesis 3). He strikes down his brother, because his brother deprives him of God's favour (Genesis 4). He is reckless and arrogant enough to show disrespect to his parents (Genesis 9:20–27). Men cannot be content to be merely human (Genesis 6:1–4). Men try to make a name for themselves (Genesis 11:1–9) by immense technical achievements. This is stated by means of ancient stories, using themes very common in ancient folk-lore. The biblical writer can make use of them because he is trying to show what man really is, everywhere and at all times. And he uses each of these stories of crime und punishment to signal the presence of the Lord of creation and of mankind, who preserves man whom he made by keeping him within his bounds.

But the stories of sin and punishment which run through the history of the origins are not all that has to be said about man outside paradise and separated from God. With profound astonishment and awe, the narrator records that God not only leaves man his life but gives him the earth in trust, together with the power to procreate new life from generation to generation, for all the centuries of an open-ended future. God has blessed his creature man: and the blessing is effective, because generation follows generation. The ponderous but impressive monotony of the genealogies depicts the might of the blessing as it makes its way through the generations, bringing forth life. The simple, basic processes of human existence are there, the ever-recurring cycle of events which represents the passage of man through the ages: being born, begetting and giving birth, living through the years of a life, dying. In these genealogies the age of an individual can be given as incredibly high, up to 900 years or more. But the numbers are not to be taken literally. They signify the conviction that the early days of mankind go back much further into the past than any genealogies could ever display.

The other aspect of this vital force passed on from generation to generation is man's power of subduing the earth. The command to till the fields and to take charge of the whole earth means all human work of development – everything in the line of cultivation. And the first chapters of the Bible show very clearly how this work of cultivation means that man is trusted and charged with the progress of culture. One special feature of man's work is the way in which it thrusts forward to the expansion of life and its transmission to the future. The first chapters of the Bible speak of the discoveries and skills which are basic to civilization – the forging of metal, the building of towns, the making of musical instruments or clothing. Arts and crafts and development in general are portrayed as the command of God. They represent, in the eyes of the writer of Genesis, a way of mastering life and of exploiting its possiblities more fully, as God commanded. But the writer constantly notes the threat to man represented by his transgressing his bounds, especially in his cultural activity. The story of the tower of Babel is the great instance (Genesis 11:1–9). None the less, the technical and cultural progress of man is clearly approved of in these stories and their allusions.

In the story of the tower of Babel, which ends the history of the origins, the two elements are emphasized once more: the power of growth, given man by his creator, which makes it possible for him to spread out over the earth; and the danger which besets man in his forward and outward drive by virtue of those technical capacities which point on to the future. Man can take himself too seriously and fail to respect the bounds which reverence for the creator makes imperative.

At this point something new intervenes and another story begins. God picks out one particular man. The history launched with Abraham starts to run its course.

THE REPERCUSSIONS

THE PROMISE OF THE LAND   The patriarch Abraham had been given a goal: "the land that I will show you". And the Israelites oppressed by forced labour in Egypt had heard God's promise

> ... to bring them up out of that land
> to a good and broad land,
> a land flowing with milk and honey.
>   (Exodus 3:8)

And after many centuries, at another time of great distress, the time of the Babylonian exile, the old promise of the land is revived in the hope of the return home, as announced by the prophet Deutero-Isaiah speaking to the banished people:

> The ransomed of the Lord shall return
> and come to Zion with singing;
> everlasting joy shall be upon their heads;
> they shall obtain joy and gladness,
> and sorrow and sighing shall flee away. (Isaiah 51:11)

In the age of the patriarchs, at the beginning of Israel's life as a nation, and finally after the great political catastrophe, we hear the promise of the land. The promise illuminates the whole course of Israel's history. Israel received its land as a gift from the hands of God, and never felt itself to be the owner of the land in the sense that it had possession of it by right and that it could do as it liked with it. Here for once a people recognized throughout their whole history that their land was a trust committed to their care, something coming to them year by year from the hands of the giver, something to be constantly and gratefully acknowledged as a gift. God alone was master of the country and he remained its sole lord. He could take it away from the people, if necessary.

A message addressed to later generations in the Book of Deuteronomy explains what it meant for Israel that its land was and remained a land of promise and of gift:

> And when the Lord your God brings you into the land
> which he swore to your fathers, to Abraham, to Isaac and to Jacob,
> to give you,
> with great and goodly cities, which you did not build,
> and houses full of all good things, which you did not fill,
> and cisterns hewn out, which you did not hew,
> and vineyards and olive-trees, which you did not plant,
> and when you eat and are full,
> then take heed lest you forget the Lord,
> who brought you out of the land of Egypt,
> out of the house of bondage.
> (Deuteronomy 6:10–12)

This was the basic attitude to the land which made it possible for the people to accept the fate of banishment in the days of calamity. A people who had forgotten their God and rebelled against him had to be told by their prophets that a day could come when they would have to leave their land. In the powerful conclusion of the law of Deuteronomy, where the prospect of blessing or of curse is held out, the new exodus, the new journey into exile, is one of the threats to a sinful people (Deuteronomy 28–29). If such things could be said when the people were dwelling tranquilly in their land, one can understand how at the times of the great catastrophes even the abandonment of the land could be accepted as the will of God. Profound love of the ancestral land, thanksgiving and joy at having it, were inspired by the fact that it was God's land, given by him, promised to the patriarchs in the distant past, accepted with constant gratitude as a newly bestowed gift, in the conviction that God meant more than the land.

FROM NOMAD TO SETTLER The period in which Israel settled down to farming and city life was the spring-time of the people. It was a time of exuberance, bold enthusiasm, and glowing dreams of the future. The traditions surviving from those days are not dry and precise historical documents. They are songs and brief episodes and stories told by many voices with many variations. In the period of transition from the nomad life, Israel had to fight for the promised land. It was not simply a matter of marching in while God wiped out all their enemies. It must even be assumed that during the struggles for the land some tribes and clans were crushed, and that the remnants were absorbed into other tribes. On the other hand, we have a picture of events from a much later date, given by the Book of Joshua in its present form, which shows Israel marching into the land in serried ranks and conquering it in one mighty onslaught. But research into the early history of Israel shows that the process was different, that peaceful penetration and military operations were more or less equally divided. Other small groups first gained a foothold bit by bit in the regions not occupied by the Canaanites. Some small groups here and there were bold enough to challenge the inhabitants and conquer small pieces of territory. The most marvellous part of the process is that these different groups, which entered the land of Canaan in different ways and at different points, were fused into one people in so relatively brief a period, and that while amalgamating they not only preserved the decisive traditions of their past but made them the basis of their altered existence in the land.

It is hard to imagine the sweeping nature of the change which came over the half-nomad tribes and clans as they settled down to new and sedentary forms of life. There was a radical economic, social and cultural change, but also a deep change in the relationship with God. At the Exodus, the small group of tribes leaving Egypt had known the God Yahweh as the saviour God. The experience of deliverance at the hands of this God was extended during the desert wanderings with a series of new saving deeds: rescue from hunger and thirst, rescue from hostile attacks, rescue through the guidance which made the way through the

24

desert possible. It was an experience of God in what happened to them, in the following of God, in an encounter renewed again and again with the God who leads and saves, in a constant series of new events along the way.

But as the Israelites settled down in the land which they had been promised and which they had none the less to fight for, a completely different experience of God and a completely different relationship to him were to mark their lives. Now that they were in the land, their existence depended on the flourishing of the crops. The rhythm of life, for the individual as for the community, was determined by the succession of the year's seaons. And this meant mortal danger for the old Israel of the desert period. Israel had now to go through one of the gravest crises of its history. For in the lovely new country – the land flowing with milk and honey, the land of noble forests and valleys bright with spring flowers – there were gods, embodied in its beauty, riches and fertility. These were the ancient gods of Canaan. How could the people avoid adopting the new form of worship – the fertility rites of the Canaanite national gods – along with the new ways of life?

Recent discoveries at Ugarit (Ras Shamra), some of which are shown in this book, have given us very valuable and copious information about the pre-Israelite Canaanite religion. We now know that it was interwoven with an extremely lively, colorful and dramatic mythology, in which we also meet some of the gods frequently mentioned in the Old Testament. It was essentially a fertility cult, embodying a dramatic cycle of decline and ascent, growth and withering, life and death, impelled by the one great rhythm of the waning and waxing of vegetation, and with this, of fertility. Clearly the Old Testament is not impartial here, but firmly condemns the religion of Canaan with all that went to make it up. Now that we know this religion from its own documents and monuments, we can understand even better why the struggle between the religion of Canaan and the faith of Israel could only be a matter of life and death. For in spite of its many grim and horrifying aspects, it was an imposing religion.

In view of the recently discovered monuments of Canaanite religion, we can now at last measure the greatness of the victory that the religion of Israel then gained. The tribes of Israel, now blended into a nation, remained loyal to the God of their fathers, the one God beside whom there were no other gods, the God who had led them out of Egypt, the God of guidance and liberation. Nevertheless, a deep change took place in the ancient faith of the fathers, which the tribes had brought with them from their desert wanderings. This God now became the God of blessing, the God who bestowed fertility on the land, and on beasts and men. The vigour of Israel's faith, in these days of its early bloom, was displayed in its power to extend its growth, and also in its ability to further its previous knowledge of God in this way. During the generations in which Israel changed to a settled way of life, two fundamentally different concepts of God were combined. A faith which was capable of remarkable developments took form. The God of the desert became the God of the fertile land. The God who had guided the people on their travels became the God who guided the people by his law when they had settled down. The God of deliverance became the God of blessing. The faith of Israel was thus enabled to prove its vitality over long spans of time. In a history of constant fresh starts, with times of stability in between, the two basic aspects of God's action could be manifested – his sudden interventions and his steady stream of blessing.

In the period when Israel was settling down in the land, a historical phenomenon occurred which was peculiar to these early days – that of the "charismatic" leaders, called "judges" in the Bible. It was typical of the people's youthful vigour, inseparably linked to faith in its first bloom. The charismatic leaders represented a special form of the exercise of authority, midway between the patriarchal form of the tribal elders and that of the permanent kingship which was to go with the new state structure. This intermediate form of authority, with its suggestion almost of democracy, could last only for a short time. It was inadequate in face of the massive threats from the enemies of later years. But it goes to show none the less that there was a period lasting for some generations in the history of Israel when political power could be wielded without its being stabilized in an institution. It was an exercise of power which went hand in hand with the greatest possible degree of liberty.

From time to time a tribe or group of tribes were hard pressed by an enemy – one of the city-states of Palestine or one of the peoples on the border. Then a young man would come forward in one of these tribes and muster his clansmen and some neighbouring clans – or perhaps even whole tribes – to take common action. Such a man did not have the authority of an institution behind him. He acted simply as a man with a call. It is in this context that we have for the first time a wide and well-attested use of the word "Spirit", which was later to have such great theological importance. This, the most ancient sense of the word, was close to our "inspiration", except that God was the source of inspiration and that the inspired agent was moved by the Spirit of God. It was a quite secular, spontaneous, natural use of the word, which went with a highly effective historical phenomenon, paving the way for a young nation on its historical course. It is unfortunate that this word "Spirit", which in the older parts of the Old Testament is vital and explosive, came to have almost the opposite meaning in the later parts of the Old Testament, and then in the New. It came to mean a sort of steady state, very far from liveliness.

The story of Gideon, Judges 6–8, recounts the call of one such charismatic leader. We are caught up in the magnificent story of a young man beginning a great task, full of courage and with no thought of himself. He is in his father's wine press, threshing the wheat there to hide it from the enemy soldiers who might try to seize it. A messenger from God appears to tell him that he is to be God's instrument in saving his people from the oppression of the Midianites. This meeting with God's messenger is a contemporary way of saying that a young man, in a flash of insight, feels certain that he can do some great deed for the community to which he belongs.

In each case the call was different. The charismatic leader could come from any section of the people. In the changing circumstances, the task was always a new one. But one thing remained the same for all the charismatic leaders. When they had succeeded in mustering volunteers and in sweeping them along with them to shake off the enemy yoke, they retired from the scene and returned to their private tasks. The power given them was only on loan, as it were. They gave it back to the source from which it came.

It is a remarkable fact that there are no sagas of mythical heroes in the telling of early Israelite history. It may be said that the stories of the judges perform the function of the heroic epics, since the Book of Judges tells of heroic deeds. But there is an important difference between these deeds and the heroic epics of other peoples. At the beginning of the great Babylonian epic, we are told that Gilgamesh (the hero) invites his friend Enkidu to join him as he sets out to do great deeds and make a name for himself which will resound to his glory. This basic theme of so many heroic sagas is absent from the literature of Israel's early days. The exploits of the charismatic leaders appear in a different setting. The power which impels and strengthens them is that of the Spirit of God, who makes their exploits possible and gives them their goal.

THE PERIOD OF THE MONARCHY   The period of the Israelite kings forms in the main a tragic section of history. As a graph, it would be a curve rising slowly and then suddenly shooting upwards to stay for a short time on a height before descending gradually, despite a few brief rises, to zero.

There have been kings in all parts of the world. At a given stage of civilization, a monarchy seems to have been inevitable, and to have wrought profound changes in history. The importance of this type of government may be seen from the fact that it survives in certain forms down to the present day, though the basis of its existence has long disappeared. Its particular importance may perhaps be explained by noting that it succeeds especially in concentrating in one man the function of ruling a whole people. It arose from the amalgamation of the two basic forms of society which existed prior to kingship: the family and the state. The king and his family – that is to say, the royal dynasty – represent the extremely ancient historical framework which we know as the "genealogy". And it preserves for a new form of society, the state, the paternal authority once exercised only in the family.

The place of the kings in the history of Israel can be properly seen only in the light of the history of the monarchy in the ancient Near East, where it appeared in an amazing variety of forms. The most important were those of Egypt and of Assyria-Babylonia. Both made an extraordinary impact on history, which certainly cannot be said of the Israelite monarchy.

The most important difference between the two types of kingship may be briefly summarized as follows. The great characteristic of the kingship of the Egyptian Pharaohs is its unbroken durability. Kingship in Egypt took on a permanence and stability unrivalled throughout the history of the world. A decisive factor in this stability was the link between the king and the gods. The king was divine and thus formed the all important bond between the realm of the gods and the kingdom of Egypt, the land and its people. The permanence of the divine activity was reflected in the permanence of the kingship. And from the king, who was united with the gods, a steady flow of blessing streamed over the land and people.

The kingship in Mesopotamia, in the kingdoms of Assyria and Babylonia, ran a different course. Here too the king was linked with the world of the gods. He was the servant or the adopted son of a god. But the king's influence was basically different. It depended on the great movements of history, and rose and fell with them. Again and again, the mighty ruler of a city went from conquest to conquest and set up a powerful empire. Again and again, one of these mighty Assyrian and Babylonian empires broke up very quickly and made room for the rise of a new one.

When the kingship was established in Israel, these two great empires existed on either side of it. The outlook was never very promising. It could not compete with either of them. Even so, a monarchical form of government proved to be unavoidable. The tribes who had migrated into Palestine found themselves extremely hard pressed by the Philistines, the occupants of the coastal districts, who had entered the land about the same time. The moment came when it seemed to the tribes that only a stable central government could save them. They sent delegates to Samuel, who then held the office of judge, demanding the appointment of a king. It is a sign of the faithfulness of the records of those early times that they have preserved the memory of the critical voices then raised in warning against the kingship. And even when a king was granted to the people, to save them from the Philistine threat, the new step was not approved unanimously.

It is a special feature of the whole history of the monarchy in Israel, that critical voices were never silent from the beginning to the end. The first king, Saul, was a tragic figure. As a close examination of the narratives reveal, he probably did not merit the sweeping condemnation which he receives in the later stories, as the opposite of David. He was one of the kings who would have been given the title of "Unfortunate" in the Assyrio-Babylonian chronicles. For all his extraordinary achievements and high gifts, he was dogged by misfortune. The rise of the young David stands out brilliantly against the dark background of the catastrophe in which the reign of Saul ended. It was the rise of a "Fortunate King" who triumphed magnificently over a difficult situation; who succeeded in uniting the tribes of the North and of the South under his rule; and who conquered Jerusalem to give his kingdom an ideal centre: the Jerusalem of the royal citadel and later of the temple, the Jerusalem of the Psalms, and in later times the Jerusalem of the yearnings of the exiles. Jerusalem, the city of David, the capital of the Israelite kings at the height of their power, survived the collapse of the monarchy. It survived great spans of history and so extends into the present day.

But the great days of David's type of kingship, of the comparatively extensive realm he had conquered, were numbered. King Solomon, David's heir, no doubt succeeded in maintaining the realm and its prosperity. But the character of his rule was dangerously close to total alienation from the ancient traditions of Israel. Heavy spending, ostentation and harsh autocracy undermined the kingdom from within. As an almost necessary consequence, the "empire" of David broke up after Solomon's death. Northern Israel separated from the South (Judah), and set up an independent monarchy. The greatness of the ancient kingdom had vanished for ever. The northern kingdom with Samaria as its capital, and the southern kingdom centred on Jerusalem, succeeded in maintaining themselves for a few hundred years longer and had an eventful history. But the splendour of the early monarchy was gone, to return no more.

The tragic character of the kingship in Israel and Judah came out very clearly in the last phase of the Judaean monarchy. This was also the period of the sharpest conflict between king and prophet. The prophet Jeremiah was active under the last kings of Judah – Josiah, Jehoiakim, Jehoiachin and Zedekiah. In less than fifty years, after its last great days under the reforming king, Josiah, the fortunes of the Judaean monarchy took a sharp downward turn. Jerusalem fell for the first time in 597, and the first exiles were taken captive to Babylon. The second capture in 587 brought with it the end of the State of Judah, the end of the temple in Jerusalem, and the end of the Judaean kingdom and monarchy.

This swift fall to utter destruction had such an effect on the tiny remnants of the population of Judah and Jerusalem that they mourned Jerusalem as dead, in the "Lamentations". The downfall and interruption of the royal line seemed above all to be unbelievably painful. The horror it inspired is heard in the Lamentations:

> Our end drew near; our days were numbered;
> for our end had come.
> Our pursuers were swifter
> than the vultures in the heavens;
> they chased us on the mountains,
> they lay in wait for us in the wilderness.
> The breath of our nostrils, the Lord's anointed
> was taken in their pits,
> he of whom we said, "Under his shadow
> we shall live among the nations." (Lamentations 4:19–20)

The anomaly hardest of all to accept was that the promise of perpetual existence made to the royal line (in the prophecy of Nathan, 2 Samuel 7) seemed to have been made null and void. In the 89th Psalm, a collective lamentation, composed not long after 587, we hear the bewildered survivors debating the broken promises:

> Of old thou didst speak in a vision
> to thy faithful one, and say:
> "I have set the crown upon one who is mighty,
> I have exalted one chosen from the people.
> I have found David my servant;
> with my holy oil I have anointed him;
> so that my hand shall ever abide with him,
> my arm also shall strengthen him.
> The enemy shall not outwit him,
> the wicked shall not humble him..."
> But now thou hast cast off and rejected,
> thou art full of wrath against thy anointed.
> Thou hast renounced the covenant with thy servant;
> thou hast defiled his crown in the dust.
> (Psalm 89:19–22, 38–39)

These words reveal such shock and bewilderment that one can well understand the persistent question about the downfall of the king and the royal line. Was this really to be God's last word on the kingship of Israel? One can understand from such questions that Israel did not give up hope of a king, but looked forward to the anointed, the Messiah, the Christ. These three terms all mean the same thing – the king as anointed by God. The messianic hope goes from the end of the Davidic monarchy to the time of Jesus of Nazareth, and beyond this, in the Jewish people, down to the present day. It is not to be explained merely by the disappointment of the collapse of the Davidic kingship. The roots of the hope go deeper. The king had been promised to Israel as its deliverer. But this promise was not fulfilled in the political sovereignty of the line of David, as long as it lasted. But this could not mean that the promise was simply useless. There had to be something still to come. But the promise has to be seen in the light of the history of kingship in all its various manifestations. All over the world, kingship was related in one way or another to the gods. All over the world, at the end of government by kings, the final break came between the political and religious spheres. And here is the key to the messianic hope. It grew out of the collapse of the Jewish monarchy, a monarchy, however, which was honoured with a promise. And this means that political kingship in this world is not God's last word on the relationship between the political and the religious spheres. The religious promise is not ultimately political.

THE PROPHETS   The voice of prophecy in Israel is one of the most remarkable phenomena of human history. Messengers of the wrath of God, messengers of judgment, raised their voices for nearly two hundred years, from the last great days of the northern kingdom, Israel, to its downfall and after, from the last great days of Judah to its collapse. Prophecy did not begin with a message of judgment. Before that, there were prophecies of blessing, and this type also was tributary to various sources. And it was not absolutely unique of its kind. In the Mari Letters (from Mari, a city midway along the Euphrates) accounts have recently been found of prophetic figures who are similar in many ways to the prophets of Israel. The most important milestone in the history of Hebrew prophecy is the beginning of written prophecy, which comes with the prophet Amos. Before that we hear of the prophets only in the historical books which contain stories of the prophets and some individual sayings. Only with literary prophecy, and the prophet Amos, is judgment pronounced on the whole people of Israel. Before that only the king, or other individuals, were threatened with divine judgment.

The marvellous element is the consistent series formed by the prophets. It runs parallel to the history of the Israelite monarchy, beginning with the first king and coming to an end with the last. Each of the prophets is a highly individual figure. Some of them are wholly isolated, though some have a companion and some have a little circle of disciples. They do not form a series in which one can leave behind him a heritage which the next can use. Each of them has to begin afresh. None of them succeeded in moving the masses. None of them attained universal recognition during his lifetime. None of them was backed by an institution or had official standing. They came forward and cried out – and their call died away. The next came and there was no change. So it went on for two hundred years, and all this time each prophet in the series had to be steadfast enough to repeat the message of the nation's doom, which never materialized. One of them finally looked back at the history of prophecy and said:

> But I said, "I have laboured in vain,
> I have spent my strength for nothing and vanity."
> (Isaiah 49:4)

Humanly speaking, it is impossible to explain how one prophet came after another, again and again, to speak, warn, suffer, despair and fall silent. Humanly speaking, this endless effort of the prophets, which always failed to make the people repent, was meaningless. What fired the endeavours of the helpless men, who raised their voices in warning but could really change nothing? Prophecy does not fit into our usual categories of the history of religion or the history of man. We cannot find here the usual framework within which we limit such a movement – rise, development, peak, spread and influence. The line of the prophets, opened symbolically by Elijah as he raises his lament on Mount Horeb, closes in the time of the great catastrophe with the prophet Jeremiah, who is carried off against his will by a group of the survivors on the last flight into Egypt. The complaints of the prophet Jeremiah, which give us an appalling view of the burdens of his office, are the great documentation of the human side of prophecy.

But we can gain some idea of all that God did for his people through these prophets. If we look at a number of writings from the time of the Babylonian exile, we can see what the message of the prophets did for the survivors when it had been ratified by history itself. They could now see a meaning in the catastrophe. The prophetic message of judgment, now accepted unquestioningly, was used to build a bridge to the future. The prophets had fallen silent, one after another, with no palpable success to their credit. But their words were a seed from which new life sprang, as the prophet of the exile says, speaking of the word of God:

> It shall not return to me empty
> but it shall accomplish that which I purpose,
> and prosper in the thing for which I sent it.
> (Isaiah 55:11)

RELIGIOUS WORSHIP   The liturgical worship of God had never ceased to be offered through all the centuries, from the time the land was first occupied until the destruction of Jerusalem and of the temple. The prophets very often made sharp attacks on the religious worship of their people. Yet the attacks were never directed against the worship itself, but only against abuses and false notions attached to the sacrifices and other rites. A wrong picture is sometimes given by laying too much stress on the prophets' criticism of the liturgy. The simple fact of persistence through all these centuries has a significance which is then lost sight of.

In reality, liturgical worship had decisive importance both for the history of the people of Israel and for the life of each individual Israelite. It was so much part of the national life and of the life of the individual that it is presupposed and accepted as self-evident in all sections of the Old Testament. It should be noted that the Old Testament has no word for "religion". The term only came into use, in all languages and cultures, at a stage when religion was ceasing to be taken for granted. Until this stage was reached life was inconceivable without religion, and in ancient times this meant in practice that life was inconceivable without liturgical worship. This may be illustrated by three examples from the Old Testament.

We read in Deuteronomy 26:1–10 that the Israelite farmer is instructed to bring the first-fruits of his fields to the priest at the altar and to make a profession of faith. This creed is a summary of the history which led up to God's bestowal of the land on his people. It is the land on which the farmer can now gather his crops, and he says as he comes to the altar:

> Now I bring the first of the fruit of the ground
> which thou, O Lord, hast given me.

The text continues:

> You shall set it down before the Lord your God
> and worship before the Lord your God,
> and you shall rejoice in all the good
> which the Lord your God has given to you and to your house,
> you, and the Levite, and the sojourner who is among you.

This brings out the essential and fundamental nature of Israel's religious worship. The farmer receives the "fruit of the ground" as a gift from the hand of God. He awaits the blessing of growth from God. He brings to the altar of God the first-fruits which he owes to this blessing. He celebrates joyfully with his family, in the sight of God, the gift of the harvest. Without this liturgical offering and without this liturgical rejoicing over the gifts of God, his life and his calling as a farmer would be unthinkable. If his life consisted only of cultivating his fields and consuming the harvest, he would not find it an existence in keeping with the dignity of man. This is how his life and his work as a farmer take on human dignity or indeed the simple character of the human: along with his work and along with the enjoyment of the harvest there is something else, something special, something on a higher level. By offering the first-fruits and celebrating the gifts, he brings his everyday work and life into communion with an overriding meaning, with another and a greater with whom he thus has stable fellowship. This is how the Israelite understands divine worship or the sacred rites. It is not a strange and separate world of cults and sacred events, but the aspect of reality which alone gives his work and his everyday life its human dignity.

In the first Book of Samuel, ch. 1, we read how a man called Elkanah came with his two wives to the shrine, to offer sacrifice. One of his wives was childless. She entered the sanctuary and asked God to grant her a child. She was so upset that the priest Eli thought at first that she was drunk. But she explained how deeply troubled she was, and what she was asking of God. The priest was then able to say to her:

Go in peace,
and the God of Israel (will) grant your petition
which you have made to him.

The text goes on:

Then the woman went her way and ate,
and her countenance was no longer sad.

Here we see another aspect of divine worship in Israel. Anyone could go with all the cares
and griefs which burdened his heart, and "pour out his heart before God". But he could
also bring his joys and all his happiness to God, give voice to them, and display his joy before
God. Every Israelite, quite spontaneously and naturally, saw the cycle of his life from joy
to sorrow, from the jubilation to the laments which echoed them, as interaction between
God and man. Another dimension was given to joy and sorrow in hymns and lamentations
such as we have in the Psalter. The Psalms gave the joys and sorrows of everyday life a dignity
which raised them above the ordinary and casual. The fact that joy and pain became an artic-
ulate cry addressed to God meant that they were joined with a purpose which everyone
was aware of, without having to put it into words. This made it possible for even the loneliest
man not to feel deserted. And even the man most tempted to despair knew that ways were
kept open which no power on earth could block.

But the possibilities opened up by prayer were not confined to intimate personal issues.
Men knew that national life was also governed by a sovereign Lord. The king too knew that
he was God's servant for the sake of God's people. Once, when the city of Jerusalem was
under siege from the Assyrian king, King Hezekiah of Judah received a message from the
attacker, summoning him to surrender. The story continues (Isaiah 37:14–17):

Hezekiah received the letter from the hands of the messengers and read it;
and Hezekiah went up to the house of the Lord,
and spread it before the Lord.
And Hezekiah prayed to the Lord:
"O Lord of hosts, God of Israel,
who art enthroned above the cherubim,
thou art the God, thou alone, of all the kingdoms of the earth;
thou hast made heaven and earth.
Incline thine ear, O Lord, and hear;
open thy eyes, O Lord, and see;
and hear all the words of Sennacherib,
which he has sent to mock the living God..."

34

The meaning of Israel's worship cannot be understood if one fails to grasp the attitude which is expressed in these words of King Hezekiah. Days of national mourning were an institution in Israel. They were always proclaimed when some great calamity threatened the people and the land, either at the hands of an enemy or through a natural catastrophe. All gathered at the temple to beseech God to avert the disaster. Such an entreaty, uttered by the whole people in time of distress, could never be automatically regulated. It could never become something merely conventional, like a prayer which one could say without attending properly to the meaning of the words. These national lamentations in Israel make it clear that prayer was extremely serious, deeply rooted in real life, and fresh and spontaneous in each new situation. Such prayer could not become a formality, a mere pious practice. When we now read the collective lamentations in the Psalter, the 80th Psalm for instance, we can only admire the directness and liveliness of this way of speaking to God. The Psalm still tingles with life, as it were. This was another of the characteristics of Israel's worship: the immediacy and vivacity of what took place between God and man. It was a characteristic which made worship a necessary element of reality, a vital element of existence, which no one could or would live without.

Finally, there is another aspect which should not be forgotten in considering the religious rites of Israel. History was kept alive in these services, and its presence was an important element in the liturgy.

The confession of faith spoken by the peasant as he laid the first-fruits of his land at the altar contained the most important features of the history of the people. The psalms recalled the great deeds of God in history. In the laments, the speakers reminded God of his earlier interventions. They appealed to the God who had proved himself historically the saviour of Israel. The commandment also recalled the saviour God.

Worship in Israel was so rich in words and actions that it is impossible to present it fully here. But one must mention the two basic elements which are most conspicuous in the worship of Israel, as in that of many other peoples. These are the temple and sacrifice. Sacrifices form a part of nearly all known religions. As far back in the past as the history of mankind can be traced, sacrifice always existed. Sacrifices are a simple way of expressing the fact that a vital relationship with God means that man must both speak to God and act with regard to him. For thousands of years, this action took the form of sacrifice. There have been many types of sacrifice, and the idea has changed profoundly in the course of time. The simple original meaning of sacrifice can perhaps be best seen in a certain type, that of the first-fruits. A farmer brought the first yield of his ground to the altar; a shepherd the first lambs and kids; others the first returns of some other work. The sacrifice was thanksgiving for the gifts received, but it was also reverent acknowledgement of the giver of all goods gifts, and homage to him from whom all growth and well-being came. But this also meant that the sacrifice of the first-fruits was a sort of silent prayer for further blessing. The whole harvest was sanctified through the first-fruits laid upon the altar. When the worshipper gratefully acknowledged the blessing, he also begged for blessing in the future. This made the sacrifice part of his life. It was not just a pious practice. It was also a great moment in the life of the family and a celebration orientated to the work of the family. Farming and cattle-raising were so closely connected with sacrifice that a successful harvest and flourishing herds were unthinkable without the blessing of God which the sacrifice acknowledged.

One further point must be noted in the history of sacrifice in Israel. There were many different types of sacrifice, offered for various ends. But in later times they were combined in one type of sacrifice with one particular aim. This was the sacrifice of expiation. The whole sacrificial liturgy of the people of Israel in later times centred on making expiation for the sins of the people, the sins of the individual and of the community. The concentration of sacrifice on this function shows that a great longing for the removal of guilt and the forgiveness of God was at work. Here we can see the effects of a history in which the people's waywardness and wrong-doing weighed heavily on the conscience of the community. But it was in this very situation that the question had to be posed as to whether sacrifice was really able to expiate the guilt of the people and of the individual, to bring about forgiveness and a new beginning. The question was still being asked in the time of Jesus. It took the form of an expectation which stirred the whole people, exemplified by the words spoken by John the Baptist at his first meeting with Jesus of Nazareth: "Behold, the Lamb of God, who takes away the sin of the world" (John 1:29).

Herod's temple, in which Jesus walked and over which he wept, was built on the site of the rather miserable temple put up after the return from the Babylonian exile. This temple had also been wept over – by those who had known the ancient temple, the magnificent building of Solomon. But even Solomon's temple had not been the first in Jerusalem. Before David conquered the city, there was an ancient Canaanite sanctuary there, of which there are several traces. The story of the priest Melchizedek in Genesis 14, in which the king of Salem brings out bread and wine to Abraham and blesses him, probably refers to the ancient Canaanite sanctuary of Jerusalem. For many thousands of years the sanctuary of Jerusalem held its place through changes of religion, of political masters and overlords. The Psalms show us the profound reverence with which this sanctuary was regarded, and the love with which the whole people clung to the temple of Jerusalem:

> How lovely is thy dwelling-place, O Lord of hosts!
> My soul longs, yea, faints
> for the courts of the Lord;
> my heart and flesh sing for joy

to the living God.
Even the sparrow finds a home,
and the swallow a nest for herself,
where she may lay her young,
at thy altars, O Lord of hosts,
my King and my God.

What the temple meant for Israel may be seen from the explanation of its origin given in part of the priestly writings. Here it appears as closely associated with one of the two historic national experiences of the desert wanderings – God's appearance on Mount Sinai. According to the priestly writing, God commanded Moses to construct a new sanctuary: the "tent of meeting", a portable shrine which was to accompany the people on their way through the desert, until they reached the land of promise. It was a model of the temple to be built later in Jerusalem. The temple, by taking the place of the tent, remained in close association with the early history of the people, with the desert wanderings and the first experience of a sacred place where God appeared and spoke to them.

Temple and sacrifice were positive elements in the worship of Israel – but not so clearly and unquestionably as one might imagine. The prophets have hard things to say about both the sacrifices and the temple. In his discourse on the temple, the prophet Jeremiah announced its destruction by God himself, because it and the sacrificial worship were no longer really manifestations of sincere and whole-hearted service of God. Worship of God had been perverted to a merely human work, used by men to give themselves a sense of security against God. The destruction of the temple, foretold by Jeremiah, actually took place, bringing with it the cessation of all the sacrificial worship.

THE EXILE AND THE RETURN   In 597, and again in 587, Jerusalem was besieged and taken. After the second capture, the city and temple were completely destroyed. When a capital was destroyed in the ancient world and, with it, the temple or the cultic centre of the whole country, the catastrophe was more than merely political. Capital, monarchy and worship collapsing in common ruin meant in the eyes of the ancient world that the fellowship between the god of the country and his people was at an end. The god disappeared along with his religion. This principle was verified in thousands of instances and could have been expected to follow the destruction of Jerusalem. This was in fact what the survivors thought. The Lamentations bear vivid witness to the first impressions caused by the disaster.

But then something remarkable happened. The survivors, who could no longer offer sacrifice because the temple was destroyed, gathered together for the rites of mourning. Appalled and grieving deeply, they thought about the events which had occurred. And one thing in particular struck them. Their prophets had foretold it all. At long last, the prophets of judgment were accorded the recognition denied them in their life-time. And as the pitiable remnants of the people gradually realized that Israel was itself to blame for the disaster, they also felt convinced that their God could not have been reduced to inactivity when the kingdom fell and the temple and its liturgy were swept away. Since he himself was the judge who struck the fearful blow, executing the verdict on his people which had been proclaimed so long before, he must still be at work. He must still be the living God.

And so in their deepest misery the people learned to cling to this God, to pray to him for help, to hope that he would turn to them once more. And the very fact that something was still expected from this God meant that the chasm was bridged. Now the message of the prophet Jeremiah was studied closely, pondered, and passed on to posterity. His sayings were gathered, and then completed by the "passion narrative" of the prophet, as written down by his companion Baruch. During the exile, and in times of great distress, the historical traditions of the people were collected and made up into an extensive compilation, the "Deuteronomic history". But the real beginning of a new period in history came with a new prophetic message – the message of the unknown prophet of the exile known as Deutero-Isaiah. He was empowered to proclaim to the scattered remnant of the exiled people that God had taken pity on the misery of his people and would bring them home again:

> Comfort, comfort my people,
> says your God.
> Speak tenderly to Jerusalem,
> and cry to her
> that her time of service is ended,
> that her iniquity is pardoned,
> that she has received from the Lord's hand
> double for all her sins.
> (Isaiah 40:1–2)

With burning enthusiasm and unshakable certainty this prophet announces the return of the exiles, a new start in the homeland, and a new future. But he says that this is possible only because of a change in God. God has had mercy on his people; he has turned graciously to them once more. There are two elements in the message of Deutero-Isaiah which are new in contrast to all earlier prophecy. They point beyond the political history of the people of Israel and signal a new future. The prophet tells his countrymen that their exile is at an end. But there is something new involved. It is not Israel that is to be restored to such political power that it can conquer the Babylonians who hold it captive in exile. It is the king of another people, Cyrus of the Persians, who is chosen by God to be the liberator. God himself charges Cyrus with the task of conquering Babylon and gives him the power to do so. The deliverance of Israel is no longer to come through Israel's own weapons. For the first time, power is no longer an element in the history of the people of God. Israel is liberated but not given political might.

The other new element follows from the first. The new salvation is not confined to Israel. It is universal. Now a call can go out to the "survivors", as the prophet looks ahead to the collapse of the Babylonian empire:

> Assemble yourselves and come,
> draw near together,
> you survivors of the nations!
> ... Turn to me and be saved,
> all the ends of the earth!
> For I am God, and there is no other.
> (Isaiah 45:20, 22)

This is the breakthrough of the new universalism; the recognition that the salvation of the God of Israel is destined for all mankind. This new outlook on salvation was possible because, in the vision of the prophet in Deutero-Isaiah, the people of God are no longer engaged in the struggle for political power against other nations. They are to be the embodiment of the salvation destined for all, and they are to bring it to all.

This message is given a very special and enigmatic form in the Servant Songs of Deutero-Isaiah (Isaiah 42:1–4; 49:1–6; 50:4–9; 52:13 – 53:12). Here universal salvation is depicted as the work of the Servant of Yahweh through vicarious suffering. These are the texts of the Old Testament which suggest most clearly the story of Jesus of Nazareth, and in the New Testament the Servant Songs in Deutero-Isaiah are interpreted as referring only to Jesus. This is to underline the connexion made in the gospels between the work, passion, death and resurrection of Jesus of Nazareth and the period of prehistory, in which the Servant Songs are to be found, in the context of the Deutero-Isaiah whose preaching brings pre-exilic prophecy to an end.

THE FUTURE   The centuries after the exile were mainly coloured by expectations of the future. The time of national independence was over; the time of Davidic kingship was gone. Israel was a province of successive kingdoms. There was a last upsurge of national power under the Maccabees. But at the end of all these heroic efforts there was another catastrophe of tragic dimensions. The excavations of the mountain citadel of Masada in particular gave grim insights into the last phase of a heroic resistance against a merciless overlord.

The expectations cherished in the centuries after the exile were given a special form in "apocalyptic" literature, which represents, along with much else that might be mentioned here, the influence of postexilic Judaism. Recent studies have laid great emphasis on the contribution of apocalyptics both to the New Testament and to the western understanding of history. The apocalyptic vision of the future produced an extensive literature, of which the beginnings are to be found in the Old Testament in the visions of the prophet Zechariah, in the "apocalypse of Isaiah" (Isaiah 24–27), in the second part of Daniel, and in a large number of brief texts scattered throughout the later parts of the prophetical books. There are some major examples of this type of literature outside the Bible and it is also found in the New Testament. The "Revelation of St John" is of course "apocalyptic", as are parts of the gospels, while there are echoes of this style and form in many other texts.

Apocalyptics, which grew out of prophecy and then took its place, search for the purpose of God in history. They do not confine their questions to the fate of the people of God, but look beyond it to the future of mankind and the fate of the world. They share this universal horizon with the history of the origins (Genesis 1–11). The latter deals with the beginnings of the world and of man, the former with their end. There are therefore a number of points at which the apocalypses correspond to the first chapters of the Bible. One tells of the creation of heaven and earth, whilst the other speaks of a new heaven and a new earth. The great catastrophe which comes upon the world in the beginning (the flood, Genesis 6–9) has its counterpart in the great catastrophe at the end. And, as in the beginning, the last word is not catastrophe, but the deliverance of the favoured. The creation of man at the beginning shows him exposed to sin, pain and death. These limitations are removed in the final act. Looking at the end from this universalist perspective, the apocalyptic vision can embrace the whole of mankind and its history in a way previously unknown. For the first time, the history of man is seen as passing through great epochs. The mighty rhythm of the rise and fall of the empires is now seen as a connected sequence of great epochs, each of which has its place and purpose in world history as a whole, a history which moves on to a predestined end. This end is the lordship of God in its universally visible manifestation, in which the meaning of the epochs of world history will be revealed.

Hence the apocalyptic vision takes up once more the great lines of God's action in man and in the world, his creation – the theme of the opening of the Bible. The special history played out between God and his elect, and the people of his elect, is not an end in itself. It moves towards a goal which is not only the goal of the people of God but God's purpose for man and creation.

THE OLD TESTAMENT VIEW OF MAN

MAN AS CREATED

Man is one among other creatures. In the Old Testament this means much more than it does in our present day thinking and feeling. In the course of western history, the simple contrast between creator and creature was gradually replaced by the contrast between man and nature. As man became the measure of all things, nature became the real object of his thoughts and energies, while God was felt to be far away in the realm of the transcendent.

In the Old Testament, the notion of man as a creature in a created world was not something that had to be taught or revealed. It was the normal way of thinking. We speak of belief in creation, and of believing in God the creator. Faith is never mentioned in the Old Testament in the texts which speak of the creator and creation. It is not something in which one can believe or not. It is rather in the nature of an axiom presupposed by all thought. The consciousness of existing brought with it at once the sense of being created.

And the world around man could be seen only as a created world. To affirm that the world was created was not a mere intellectual proposition. It was part of real life, since the world was in the same situation as man before God and had to partake in man's joy as he turned in worship to God:

> Praise him, sun and moon,
> praise him, all you shining stars!
> Praise the Lord from the earth,
> you sea monsters and all deeps,
> fire and hail, snow and frost,
> stormy wind fulfilling his command!
> (Psalm 148:1,7)

In the exhaustion and bewilderment of the exile, the people are told to think of the creator of the stars (Isaiah 40:26–29):

Lift up your eyes on high and see:
who created these?
He who brings out their host by number,
calling them all by name...
Have you not known? Have you not heard?
The Lord is the everlasting God,
the Creator of the ends of the earth.
He does not faint or grow weary,
his understanding is unsearchable.
He gives power to the faint,
and to him who has no might he increases strength.

When the Old Testament says that man is created, it is not offering a theory or some information about his origin. It enunciates man's self-understanding, which is based on his standing before God. It is only in the eyes of God that he is anything:

When I look at thy heavens, the work of thy fingers,
the moon and the stars which thou hast established;
what is man that thou art mindful of him,
and the son of man that thou dost care for him?
Yet thou hast made him little less than God,
and dost crown him with glory and honour.
Thou hast given him dominion over the works of thy hands.
(Psalm 8)

The truth that man is God's creature and hence that his whole life is enveloped by God is given particularly beautiful expression in the 139th Psalm:

O Lord, thou hast searched me and known me!
Thou knowest when I sit down and rise up;
thou discernest my thoughts from afar.
Thou searchest out my path and my lying down,
and art acquainted with all my ways.
Even before a word is on my tongue,
lo, O Lord, thou knowest it altogether...
Such knowledge is too wonderful for me;
it is high, I cannot attain it.

When the singer of this psalm says, "thou art acquainted with all my ways", he means his everyday life, his ordinary preoccupations and his work, and all that goes with them. He is not analysing the "essence of man". Man, as God's creature, is always the individual, particular man, this man or that woman or that child. He has his own name, his own bodily stature with his own gifts or defects, with his hunger and thirst, his questions and desires, his laughter and tears, his own special gestures and the thoughts that are his alone.

MAN POISED BETWEEN BIRTH AND DEATH

Mans's life as God's creature stretches like an arc between the poles of birth and death: "For you are dust, and to dust you shall return." Every age of human life has its own essential function, and the only sound community is one which includes old people and children. Here it should be noted that the structure of the family in Old Testament times was different from what it is now. The generations were much closer together, because the marriage age was lower. And then the economy was purely agrarian, which made it possible for the members of the family to remain in closer proximity. Another important feature was the attitude of the older to the younger members. It was not authoritarian, as is so often imagined. Old and young were joined together by the blessing. The older members, even the very old, had something to give the young which the latter could only obtain through the blessing which came from the former. By blessing is meant all that God has brought to maturity in a human life. It includes experience – but it is more than experience. Reverence for parents was based on the fact that they were in a position to pass on such a blessing. Authority was not a personal possession which one had therefore to claim. It was rather the acknowledgment of a force which was effective as it passed from generation to generation. Authority went with this force, but not with age as such, or with old men as such.

This also helps us to understand what the Bible means by wisdom. Wisdom is where the blessing takes effect. Wisdom is something that can come only through ripeness.

But youth also has its own definite place in the Old Testament. The enthusiasm and spontaneous exuberance of youth is as much part of life as the wisdom of the mature. The Book of Judges is a young nation's book and is clearly marked by the fresh vigour of youth. And the story of the kings is also to a great extent the story of the deeds and inspiration of young men.

In all the Old Testament narratives, man is taken seriously at any given stage of his life. The relationship of God to a young man is not the same as to an older man. Since God takes in the whole of life, a child's link with God is different from that of a man in the evening of life. For the same reason, death in the Old Testament is viewed in terms of the full course of a man's life. It is by no means the same thing that a young man is taken from among the living, in the prime of life, and that an old man dies, "full of years", well satisfied with his long span. In the Old Testament, death is not regarded as coming only at the end of life. It is a power which makes itself felt throughout life. Its power is described in a text of the Book of Job:

Man that is born of woman
is of few days, and full of trouble.
He comes forth like a flower, and withers;
he flees like a shadow, and continues not...
For there is hope for a tree,
if it be cut down, that it will sprout again,
and that its shoots will not cease.
Though its root grow old in the earth,
and its stump die in the ground,
yet at the scent of water it will bud
and put forth branches like a young plant.
But man dies, and is laid low;
man breathes his last, and where is he?
(Job 14:1–2, 7–10)

But this knowledge of death and its power is counterbalanced by a radiant joy at being alive, as in the psalm of King Hezekiah, which begins with a lament for his illness and ends in a burst of praise:

Lo, it was for my welfare
that I had great bitterness;
but thou hast held back my life
from the pit of destruction...
For Sheol cannot thank thee,
death cannot praise thee...
The living, the living, he thanks thee as I do this day.
(Isaiah 38:17–19)

That the joy of being alive takes the form of praise of God is highly characteristic of the view of man found in the Old Testament. The praise of God is simply the joy of life put into words.

MAN'S WORK

Throughout the Old Testament work is taken to be part of man's existence. It is the labour of the farmer, the herdsman, or the artisan, in a poor country and on stony ground. In the narrative account of the creation of man God charges his creature to tend and till the earth. Along with space to live in and the provision of nourishment, work is one of the gifts of creation. Hence a life without it would not be a life fit for man. Two aspects are mentioned in connexion with man's work. He is the cultivator and the custodian of the earth. This means that all types of work are included, as man cultivates and cherishes what he knows is entrusted to him by God. But the same story says something else about the field of man's work: " Thorns and thistles it shall bring forth to you ... In the sweat of your face you shall eat bread." It would be a gross error to think that all work is cursed in this denunciation of the earth. Behind the saying is the conviction that in one way or another all man's work involves thorns and thistles; that the ideal job simply does not exist; and that happiness cannot be manufactured. But this does not change the fact that before man disobeyed he was charged by God to till and tend the earth. All work worthy of man, whatever form it takes, is done at God's command, as part of the task set men on earth.

But God's commandment, as here propounded, is not confined to work as such. Work is development, and development is part of the blessing. In the stories of the origins, progress in invention and achievement is part of man's work. The progress of human work in science and technology is clearly attributed to the blessing of the creator.

But these general statements of the Bible are supplemented by the law of the division of labour. This is shown to be operative at the beginning of all human development, and its importance is recognized. The division of labour begins with Cain and Abel, the children of the first human couple. Each takes up one of the basic callings of a given period of civilization: farming and cattle-raising. The stories show that conflicts arose at once with the division of labour. They recur in the story of Jacob and Esau.

In a later text, the problem raised by differences between the various types of work come clearly to the fore. At the time of the establishment of the monarchy in Israel, there were groups who opposed this development. Their polemics against the innovation which the monarchy represented is reflected in the fable recounted by Jotham (Judges 9), which contemptuously contrasts the haughtiness of the king with the regular work of those engaged in useful production. This represents the dislike of the independent farmer for the new form of stable rule:

> The trees once went forth to anoint a king over them;
> and they said to the fig tree,

"Come you, and reign over us". But the fig tree said to them,
"Shall I leave my sweetness and my good fruit, and go to
sway over the trees?"

The trees try other useful trees, and all refuse to become king. But when they come to the useless thornbush, it agrees at once.

The technical achievement of opening up progressively new fields of work is also praised in the Old Testament. The twenty-eight chapter of the Book of Job reflects one of the great technical discoveries of man, the mining of metals in the depths of the earth. One can sense at once the admiration and joy at this human achievement:

Surely there is a mine for silver,
and a place for gold which they refine.
Iron is taken out of the earth,
and copper is smelted from the ore.
Men put an end to darkness,
and search out to the farthest bound
the ore in gloom and deep darkness.

Finally, the Old Testament recognizes the special place of intellectual activity and treasures it highly. Even in early times the sage, like the prince, priest and prophet, was considered to belong to the leading classes. The Books of Kings include short historical works, such as the story of David's rise to power and the succession narrative, which are among the finest pieces of historical writing in antiquity.

On the very periphery of the Old Testament, in the Book of Ecclesiastes (the preacher), the concept of methodical enquiry, the questioning survey of all beings, is considered, but approached with profound scepticism:

When I applied my mind to know wisdom
and to see the business that is done on earth...
then I saw all the work of God, that man cannot find out
the work that is done under the sun.
However much man may toil in seeking,
he will not find it out...
All this I have tested by wisdom;
I said, "I will be wise"; but it was far from me.
That which is, is far off, and deep, very deep;
who can find it out?

MAN IN SOCIETY

In the Old Testament, man does not first appear as an individual who then goes on to form a community. From the start he is part of a sort of community. In the story of the creation of man there is a remarkable statement, to the effect that God has made man but is not satisfied with the result of his work. The being which has been created is not really man as he was meant to be. "It is not good that man should be alone; I will make him a helper fit for him." This is a simple narrative way of saying that only in fellowship with other men is man the creature really intended by God. Man is created for fellowship. In the creation story, the companionship of man and woman is mentioned as the basis of all human society. The meaning is that man only finds his true nature in society.

The relation of the individual to the community cannot be determined once and for all. It changes with the passage of history. In the Old Testament, the fundamental form of human society is the family. In Genesis, the stories of the patriarchs depict the basic relationships of human society, as manifested in the family, in the light of a tradition covering hundreds of years. A large number of simple human traits which are always part of human nature have been woven into the narratives. The stories of the patriarchs show how a man gets his nature and his character from the family. All that goes on in the passage of history, and all that is depicted in the writing of history, is to some extent basically determined by these simple human relationships. The protagonists of history are first and foremost sons and brothers, husbands and fathers, sisters or morthers.

The story of Abraham shows a father being exposed to a severe and almost superhuman test. The conversation between the father and the son on the way (Genesis 22:6–8) brings out the greatness of this hour. A mother, one of the wives of Saul, disregards the king's command and watches over the bodies of her dead sons, until they are buried (2 Sam 11:9–10). A brother is ready to forfeit his freedom for the sake of his younger brother, for whom he is responsible to his father (Genesis 44:30–34).

The Israelite, involved in the history of his people, could not but be involved in the drama played out between this people and God. This relationship changed in each epoch, demanding constant reappraisals and new decisions. The Old Testament shows an extraordinarily quick succession of forms of society: family and clan, nomadic groups, a tribal federation in the process of establishment, the setting up of a state, the monarchy, and the religious fellowship of a province. All these were steps along the way of a people and its God. The historical continuity which links these very different phases is based on the encounter between God and the people which runs through it all – and which the Old Testament calls the covenant. The dialogue signified by the word "covenant" began with God's deliverance, his guidance, protection and blessing. Then came the drama of the people's disobedience: a history of growing culpability which led to God's judgment on his people.

Here at the end there is a new departure. Individuals stand out, one after another, in the ranks of the prophets, to oppose the way of the people. At the end of the series comes Jeremiah, the suffering prophet, and then, pointing on into the future, the servant of the Lord who suffers vicariously for the whole people.

THE LORD SAID TO ABRAM…

Now the Lord said to Abram, "Go from your country and your kindred and your father's house to the land that I will show you. And I will make of you a great nation, and I will bless you, and make your name great, so that you will be a blessing. I will bless those who bless you, and him who curses you I will curse; and by you all the families of the earth shall bless themselves."

So Abram went, as the Lord had told him; and Lot went with him. Abram was seventy-five years old when he departed from Haran. And Abram took Sarai his wife, and Lot his brother's son, and all their possessions which they had gathered, and the persons that they had gotten in Haran; and they set forth to go to the land of Canaan. When they had come to the land of Canaan, Abram passed through the land to the place at Shechem, to the oak of Moreh. At that time the Canaanites were in the land. Then the Lord appeared to Abram, and said, "To your descendants I will give this land." So he built there an altar to the Lord, who had appeared to him. Thence he removed to the mountain on the east of Bethel, and pitched his tent, with Bethel on the west and Ai on the east; and there he built an altar to the Lord and called on the name of the Lord. And Abram journeyed on, still going toward the Negeb.

Genesis 12:1–9

Right: Shepherd, clay statuette of the period when Abram set out on his way to Canaan.
Following pages: The mountains of the Negeb, the southern desert.

And Sarah conceived, and bore Abraham a son in his old age at the time of which God had spoken to him. Abraham called the name of his son who was born to him, whom Sarah bore him, Isaac. And Abraham circumcised his son Isaac when he was eight days old, as God had commanded him. Abraham was a hundred years old when his son Isaac was born to him.   *Genesis 21:2–5*

Abraham was the father of Isaac, and Isaac was forty years old when he took to wife Rebekah, the daughter of Bethuel the Aramean of Paddan-aram, the sister of Laban the Aramean. When her days to be delivered were fulfilled, behold, there were twins in her womb. The first came forth red, all his body like a hairy mantle; so they called his name Esau. Afterward his brother came forth, and his hand had taken hold of Esau's heel; so his name was called Jacob. Isaac was sixty years old when she bore them.

Genesis 25:20, 24–26

Jacob left Beer-sheba, and went toward Haran. And he came to a certain place, and stayed there that night. And he dreamed that there was a ladder set up on the earth, and the top of it reached to heaven; and behold, the angels of God were ascending and descending on it! And behold, the Lord stood above it and said, "I am the Lord, the God of Abraham your father and the God of Isaac; the land on which you lie I will give to you and to your descendants; and your descendants shall be like the dust of the earth, and you shall spread abroad to the west and to the east and to the north and to the south; and by you and your descendants shall all the families of the earth bless themselves. Behold, I am with you and will keep you wherever you go, and will bring you back to this land; for I will not leave you until I have done that of which I have spoken to you."

Genesis 28:10–15

So Jacob said to his household and to all who were with him, "Put away the foreign gods that are among you, and purify yourselves, and change your garments; then let us arise and go up to Bethel, that I may make there an altar to the God who answered me in the day of my distress and has been with me wherever I have gone." So they gave to Jacob all the foreign gods that they had, and the rings that were in their ears; and Jacob hid them under the oak which was near Shechem.   *Genesis 35:2–4*

Left: Fertility goddesses, clay figurines of the kind hidden by Jacob under the oak near Shechem.

Joseph was thirty years old when he entered the service of Pharaoh king of Egypt. And Joseph went out from the presence of Pharaoh, and went through all the land of Egypt. Moreover, all the earth came to Egypt to Joseph to buy grain, because the famine was severe over all the earth.

Genesis 41:46, 57

Then Jacob set out from Beer-sheba; and the sons of Israel carried Jacob their father, their little ones, and their wives, in the wagons which Pharaoh had sent to carry him. They also took their cattle and their goods, which they had gained in the land of Canaan, and came into Egypt, Jacob and all his offspring with him, his sons, and his sons' sons with him, his daughters, and his sons' daughters; all his offspring he brought with him into Egypt.

Genesis 46:5–7

Then Joseph died, and all his brothers, and all that generation. But the descendants of Israel were fruitful and increased greatly; they multiplied and grew exceedingly strong; so that the land was filled with them.

Now there arose a new king over Egypt, who did not know Joseph. And he said to his people, "Behold, the people of Israel are too many and too mighty for us." So they made the people of Israel serve with rigor, and made their lives bitter with hard service, in mortar and brick, and in all kinds of work in the field; in all their work they made them serve with rigor.

Exodus 1:6–9, 13–14

Then the Lord said, "I have seen the affliction of my people who are in Egypt, and have heard their cry because of their taskmasters; I know their sufferings, and I have come down to deliver them out of the hand of the Egyptians, and to bring them up out of that land."

Exodus 3:7–8

Right: A Semite family asking permission to go to Egypt, Egyptian tomb fresco.
Following pages: Two men in the position of respect Moses and Aaron would have adopted before Pharaoh.
Basalt statue of Ramses II, during whose reign the Israelites left Egypt.
Galloping horses, clay relief. This picture symbolizes the swiftness of the Egyptian war-chariot regiment.

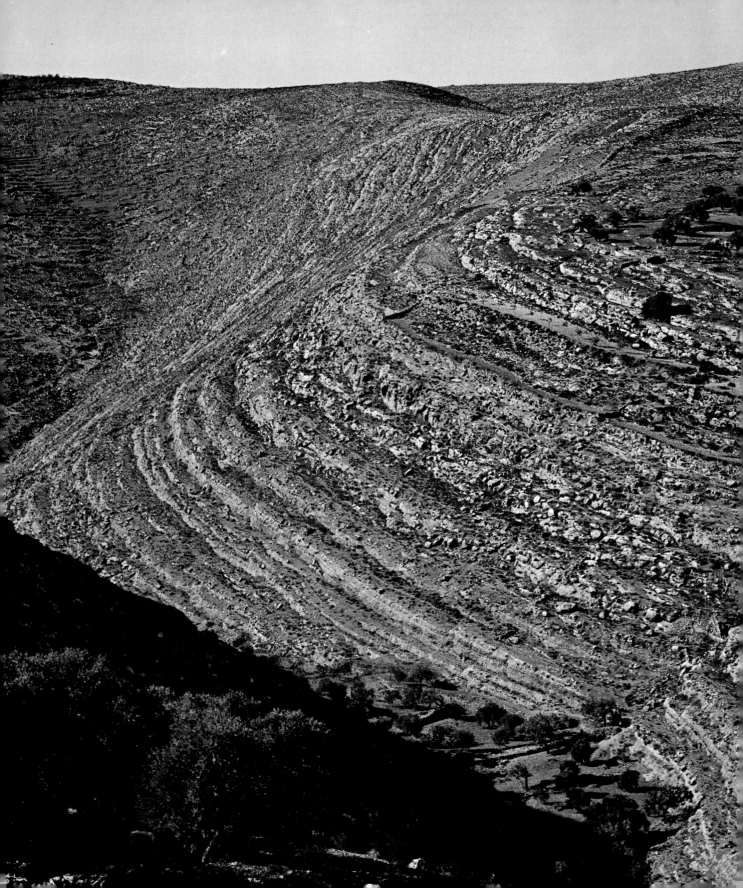

The Lord said to Moses, "Send men to spy out the land of Canaan, which I give to the people of Israel; from each tribe of their fathers shall you send a man, every one a leader among them." At the end of forty days they returned from spying out the land. And they told him, "We came to the land to which you sent us; it flows with milk and honey, and this is its fruit. Yet the people who dwell in the land are strong, and the cities are fortified and very large."

Numbers 13:1–2, 25, 27–28

Then all the congregation raised a loud cry; and the people wept that night. And all the people of Israel murmured against Moses and Aaron; the whole congregation said to them, "Would that we had died in the land of Egypt! Or would that we had died in this wilderness!"

Numbers 14:1–2

Then the Lord said, "And none of those who despised me shall see the land which I swore to give to their fathers. Your dead bodies shall fall in this wilderness; and of all your number, numbered from twenty years old and upward, who have murmured against me, not one shall come into the land where I swore that I would make you dwell. And your chil-dren shall be shepherds in the wilderness forty years, and shall suffer for your faithlessness, until the last of your dead bodies lies in the wilderness. According to the number of the days in which you spied out the land, forty days, for every day a year, you shall bear your iniquity, forty years, and you shall know my displeasure."

Numbers 14:23, 29–30, 33–34

From Mount Hor they set out by the way to the Red Sea, to go around the land of Edom; and the people became im-patient on the way. Then the Lord sent fiery serpents among the people, and they bit the people, so that many people of Israel died. And the people came to Moses, and said, "We have sinned, for we have spoken against the Lord and against you; pray to the Lord, that he take away the serpents from us." So Moses prayed for the people. And the Lord said to Moses, "Make a fiery serpent, and set it on a pole; and every one who is bitten, when he sees it, shall live." So Moses made a bronze serpent, and set it on a pole; and if a serpent bit any man, he would look at the bronze serpent and live. *Numbers 21:4, 6–9*

Preceding pages: The Jordan, with the Gilead range. Here the Israelites crossed the river.
Hittite soldier with trumpet. Similar trumpets and horns may have been used when the Israelite warriors stormed the walls of Jericho.
Left: Rocky terraces (Shebarim) near Ai, where Joshua's troops experienced defeat and victory.

After the death of Moses the servant of the Lord, the Lord said to Joshua the son of Nun, Moses' minister, "Moses my servant is dead; now therefore arise, go over this Jordan, you and all this people, into the land which I am giving to them, to the people of Israel." *Joshua 1:1–2*

And Joshua the son of Nun sent two men secretly from Shittim as spies, saying, "Go, view the land, especially Jericho." Then the two men came down again from the hills, and passed over and came to Joshua the son of Nun; and they told him all that had befallen them. And they said to Joshua, "Truly the Lord has given all the land into our hands; and moreover all the inhabitants of the land are fainthearted because of us." *Joshua 2:1, 23–24*

So, when the people set out from their tents, to pass over the Jordan with the priests bearing the ark of the covenant before the people.... *Joshua 3:14*

And the Lord said to Joshua, "See, I have given into your hand Jericho, with its king and mighty men of valor. You shall march around the city, all the men of war going around the city once. Thus shall you do for six days. And seven priests shall bear seven trumpets of rams' horns before the ark; and on the seventh day you shall march around the city seven times, the priests blowing the trumpets. And when they make a long blast with the ram's horn, as soon as you hear the sound of the trumpet, then all the people shall shout with a great shout; and the wall of the city will fall down flat." *Joshua 6:2–5*

Joshua sent men from Jericho to Ai, which is near Beth-aven, east of Bethel, and said to them, "Go up and spy out the land." And the men went up and spied out Ai. So about three thousand went up there from the people; and they fled before the men of Ai, and the men of Ai killed about thirty-six men of them, and chased them before the gate as far as Shebarim, and slew them at the descent. And the hearts of the people melted, and became as water. *Joshua 7:2, 4–5*

And the Lord said to Joshua, "Do not fear or be dismayed; take all the fighting men with you, and arise, go up to Ai; see, I have given into your hand the king of Ai and his people, his city, and his land; and you shall do to Ai and its king as you did to Jericho and its king." *Joshua 8:1–2*

When Adoni-zedek king of Jerusalem heard how Joshua had taken Ai, and had utterly destroyed it, doing to Ai and its king as he had done to Jericho and its king and how the inhabitants of Gibeon had made peace with Israel and were among them, he feared greatly, because Gibeon was a great city, like one of the royal cities, and because it was greater than Ai, and all its men were mighty. So Adoni-zedek king of Jerusalem sent to Hoham king of Hebron, to Piram king of Jarmuth, to Japhia king of Lachish, and to Debir king of Eglon, saying, "Come up to me, and help me, and let us smite Gibeon; for it has made peace with Joshua and with the people of Israel." So Joshua came upon them suddenly, having marched up all night from Gilgal. And the Lord threw them into a panic before Israel, who slew them with a great slaughter at Gibeon, and chased them by the way of the ascent of Beth-horon, and smote them as far as Azekah and Makkedah. Then spoke Joshua to the Lord in the day when the Lord gave the Amorites over to the men of Israel; and he said in the sight of Israel,

"Sun, stand thou still at Gibeon,
and thou Moon in the valley of Aijalon."
And the sun stood still, and the moon stayed,
until the nation took vengeance on their enemies.

Is this not written in the Book of Jashar? The sun stayed in the midst of heaven, and did not hasten to go down for about a whole day. There has been no day like it before or since, when the Lord hearkened to the voice of a man; for the Lord fought for Israel.

Then Joshua returned, and all Israel with him, to the camp at Gilgal. *Joshua 10:1–4, 9–10, 12–15*

So Joshua took the whole land, according to all that the Lord had spoken to Moses; and Joshua gave it for an inheritance to Israel according to their tribal allotments. And the land had rest from war. *Joshua 11:23*

So Joshua made a covenant with the people that day, and made statutes and ordinances for them at Shechem. And Joshua wrote these words in the book of the law of God; and he took a great stone, and set it up there under the oak in the sanctuary of the Lord. And Joshua said to all the people, "Behold, this stone shall be a witness against us; for it has heard all the words of the Lord which he spoke to us; therefore it shall be a witness against you, lest you deal falsely with your God."   *Joshua 24: 25–27*

And the people of Israel did what was evil in the sight of the Lord and served the Baals; and they forsook the Lord, the God of their fathers, who had brought them out of the land of Egypt; they went after other gods, from among the gods of the peoples who were round about them, and bowed down to them.

Then the Lord raised up judges, who saved them out of the power of those who plundered them. And yet they did not listen to their judges; for they played the harlot after other gods and bowed down to them. And the Lord sold them into the hand of Jabin king of Canaan, who reigned in Hazor; the commander of his army was Sisera, who dwelt in Harosheth-ha-goiim.   *Judges 2: 11–12, 16–17; 4: 2*

Now Deborah, a prophetess, the wife of Lappidoth, was judging Israel at that time. She sent and summoned Barak the son of Abino-am from Kedesh in Naphtali, and said to him, "The Lord, the God of Israel, commands you, 'Go, gather your men at Mount Tabor, taking ten thousand from the tribe of Naphtali and the tribe of Zebulun. And I will draw out Sisera, the general of Jabin's army, to meet you by the river Kishon with his chariots and his troops; and I will give him into your hand.'"

So Barak went down from Mount Tabor with ten thousand men following him. And the Lord routed Sisera and all his chariots and all his army before Barak at the edge of the sword; and Sisera alighted from his chariot and fled away on foot. And Barak pursued the chariots and the army to Harosheth-ha-goiim, and all the army of Siera fell by the edge of the sword; not a man was left.

Judges 4: 4, 6–7, 14–16

Right: Valley of Aijalon, seen from Gibeon. Here Joshua defeated the armies of the five kings of the Amorites.
Following pages: A sacred stone in the ruins of the ancient site of Shechem.
Male head, probably Canaanite in origin.
Archer in a war-chariot of the kind which Sisera used against the Israelites. Relief on a golden bowl.

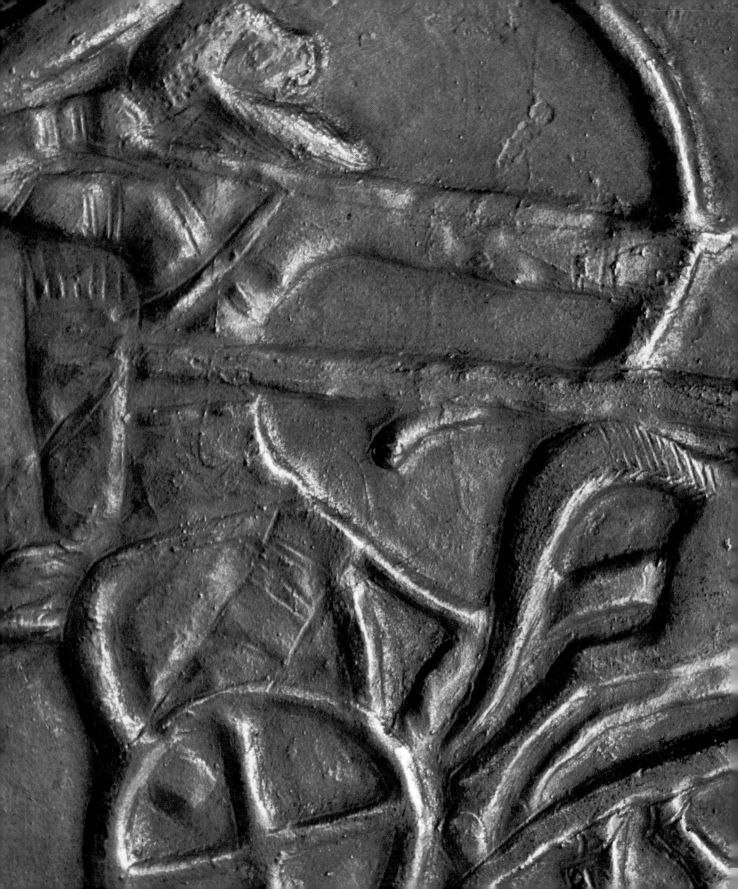

The people of Israel did what was evil in the sight of the Lord; and the Lord gave them into the hand of Midian seven years. And the hand of Midian prevailed over Israel.

Judges 6: 1–2

Now the angel of the Lord came and said to Gideon: "Deliver Israel from the hand of Midian; do not I send you? Pull down the altar of Baal which your father has, and cut down the Asherah that is besides it; and build an altar to the Lord your God on the top of the stronghold here." Therefore on that day he was called Jerubbaal, that is to say, "Let Baal contend against him," because he pulled down his altar.

Judges 6: 11, 14, 25–26, 32

Then all the Midianites and the Amalekites and the people of the East came together, and crossing the Jordan they encamped in the Valley of Jezreel. Then Jerubbaal (that is, Gideon) and all the people who were with him rose early and encamped beside the spring of Harod; and the camp of Midian was north of them, by the hill of Moreh, in the valley. The Lord said to Gideon, "The people with you are too many for me to give the Midianites into their hand, lest Israel vaunt themselves against me, saying, 'My own hand has delivered me.' Now therefore proclaim in the ears of the people, saying, 'Whoever is fearful and trembling, let him return home.'" And Gideon tested them; twenty-two thousand returned, and ten thousand remained.

And the Lord said to Gideon, "The people are still too many; take them down to the water and I will test them for you there. So he brought the people down to the water; and the Lord said to Gideon, "Every one that laps the water with his tongue, as a dog laps, you shall set by himself; likewise every one that kneels down to drink." And the number of those that lapped, putting their hands to their mouths, was three hundred men. And the Lord said to Gideon, "With the three hundred men that lapped I will deliver you, and give the Midianites into your hand."

And as Gideon with his three hundred men approached the camp, the Lord set every man's sword against his fellow and against all the army; and the army fled as far as Beth-shittah toward Zereah, as far as the border of Abel-meholah, by Tabbath.

Judges 6: 33; 7: 1–7, 22

So Midian was subdued before the people of Israel, and they lifted up their heads no more. And the land had rest forty years in the days of Gideon.

Judges 8: 28

Preceding pages: The goddess Astarte, a popular Canaanite divinity.
The cave in which the spring of Harod rises.
The fertile plain of Jezreel, with the hill of Moreh and Mount Tabor in the background. Here Gideon defeated the army of Midian.
Left: A sacrificial altar of the kind in use in the time of Gideon.

87

In those days Samuel grew, and the Lord was with him and let none of his words fall to the ground. And all Israel from Dan to Beer-sheba knew that Samuel was established as a prophet of the Lord. And the Lord appeared again at Shiloh, for the Lord revealed himself to Samuel at Shiloh by the word of the Lord. And the word of Samuel came to all Israel. *1 Samuel 3:19–21, 4:1*

Samuel judged Israel all the days of his life. And he went on a circuit year by year to Bethel, Gilgal, and Mizpah; and he judged Israel in all these places. Then he would come back to Ramah, for his home was there, and there also he administered justice to Israel. And he built there an altar to the Lord. *1 Samuel 7:15–17*

When Samuel became old, then all the elders of Israel gathered together and came to Samuel at Ramah, and said to him, "Behold, you are old and your sons do not walk in your ways; now appoint for us a king to govern us like all the nations." But the thing displeased Samuel. *1 Samuel 8:1,4–6*

There was a man of Benjamin whose name was Kish, the son of Abiel, son of Zeror, son of Becorath, son of Aphiah, a Benjaminite, a man of wealth; and he had a son whose name was Saul, a handsome young man. There was not a man among the people of Israel more handsome than he; from his shoulders upward he was taller than any of the people.

When Samuel saw Saul, the Lord told him, "Here is the man of whom I spoke to you! He it is who shall rule over my people."

Then Samuel took a vial of oil and poured it on his head, and kissed him and said, "Has not the Lord anointed you to be prince over his people Israel? And you shall reign over the people of the Lord and you will save them from the hand of their enemies round about. And this shall be the sign to you that the Lord has anointed you to be prince over his heritage. *1 Samuel 9:1–2,17; 10:1*

When Saul had taken the kingship over Israel, he fought against all his enemies on every side, against Moab, against the Ammonites, against Edom, against the kings of Zobah, and against the Philistines; wherever he turned he put them to the worse. And he did valiantly, and smote the Amalekites, and delivered Israel out of the hands of those who plundered them. *1 Samuel 14:47–48*

Now the Spirit of the Lord departed from Saul, and an evil spirit from the Lord tormented him. One of the young men answered, "Behold, I have seen David, a son of Jesse the Bethlehemite, who is skilful in playing, a man of valor, a man of war, prudent in speech, and a man of good presence; and the Lord is with him." *1 Samuel 16:14,18*

Right: The hill of Ramah, still known as the "Hill of Samuel," where Samuel refused to appoint a king, and where later Saul was anointed.
Following pages: Ivory horn ornamented with gold bands, possibly used for anointing a king.
A young man plays the lyre before a king on his throne. Engraved ivory tablet.
Head of a Philistine, Egyptian stone relief.
The Valley of Elah, with the hills of Socoh and Azekah in the background. Here the Israelites and David fought against the Philistines.

In the morning David wrote a letter to Joab, and sent it by the hand of Uriah. In the letter he wrote, "Set Uriah in the forefront of the hardest fighting, and then draw back from him, that he may be struck down, and die."

2 Samuel 11:14

And the Lord struck the child that Uriah's wife bore to David, and it died. Then David comforted his wife, Bathsheba, and went in to her, and lay with her; and she bore a son, and he called his name Solomon. And the Lord loved him.

2 Samuel 12:15, 24

And David won a name for himself. He slew eighteen thousand Edomites in the Valley of Salt. And he put garrisons in Edom; throughout all Edom he put garrisons, and all the Edomites became David's servants. And the Lord gave victory to David wherever he went.
So David reigned over all Israel; and David administered justice and equity to all his people.   *2 Samuel 8:13–15*

When David's time to die drew near, he charged Solomon his son, saying, "I am about to go the way of all the earth. Be strong, and show yourself a man, and keep the charge of the Lord your God, walking in his ways and keeping his statutes, his commandments, his ordinances, and his testimonies, as it is written in the law of Moses, that you may prosper in all that you do and wherever you turn.
Then David slept with his fathers, and was buried in the city of David. And the time that David reigned over Israel was forty years; he reigned seven years in Hebron, and thirty-three years in Jerusalem. So Solomon sat upon the throne of David his father; and his kingdom was firmly established.   *1 Kings 2:1–3, 10–12*

Preceding pages: Bronze statuette of a Hittite warrior.
Soldiers on a tower, engraved copper vessel from the time of King David.
Left: The Valley of Salt (Dead Sea) where David overcame the Edomites.

The people were sacrificing at the high places, however, because no house had yet been built for the name of the Lord. Solomon loved the Lord, walking in the statutes of David his father; only, he sacrificed and burnt incense at the high places.   *1 Kings 3: 2–3*

Solomon ruled over all the kingdoms from the Eu-phrates to the land of the Philistines and to the border of Egypt; they brought tribute and served Solomon all the days of his life.

Now Hiram king of Tyre sent his servants to Solomon. And Solomon sent word to Hiram: "I purpose to build a house for the name of the Lord my God, as the Lord said to David my father, 'Your son, whom I will set upon your throne in your place, shall build the house for my name.' Now therefore command that cedars of Lebanon be cut for me." And Hiram sent to Solomon, saying, "I have heard the message which you have sent to me; I am ready to do all you desire in the matter of cedar and cypress timber. My servants shall bring it down to the sea from Lebanon; and I will make it into rafts to go by sea to the place you direct."
1 Kings 4: 21; 5: 1–2, 5–6, 8–9

In the four hundred and eightieth year after the people of Israel came out of the land of Egypt, in the fourth year of Solomon's reign over Israel, in the month of Ziv, which is the second month, he began to build the house of the Lord. In the inner sanctuary Solomon made two cherubim of olive-wood, each ten cubits high. He put the cherubim in the innermost part of the house; and the wings of the cherubim were spread out so that a wing of one touched the one wall, and a wing of the other cherub touched the other wall; their other wings touched each other in the middle of the house.   *1 Kings 6: 1, 23, 27*

And King Solomon sent and brought Hiram from Tyre. He was full of wisdom, understanding, and skill, for making any work in bronze. Hiram made the molten sea; it was round, ten cubits from brim to brim, and five cubits high, and a line of thirty cubits measured its circumference. Under its brim were gourds, for thirty cubits, compassing the sea round about; the gourds were in two rows, cast with it when it was cast.   *1 Kings 7: 13–14, 23–24*

Right: Offering at a "high place," bronze model.
Following pages: Cedars from Lebanon were shipped by sea. Stone relief.
Ivory statuette of a cherub. Solomon had two of these mythical winged animals placed in the Temple.
Three-legged support for a ceremonial basin, hung with pomegranates. Hiram of Tyre made similar stands for the Temple of Solomon.

King Solomon built a fleet of ships at Ezion-geber, which is near Eloth on the shore of the Red Sea, in the land of Edom. And Hiram sent with the fleet his servants, seamen who were familiar with the sea, together with the servants of Solomon; and they went to Ophir, and brought from there gold, to the amount of four hundred and twenty talents; and they brought it to King Solomon.

1 Kings 9:26–28

Now when the queen of Sheba heard of the fame of Solomon concerning the name of the Lord, she came to test him with hard questions. She came to Jerusalem with a very great retinue, with camels bearing spices, and very much gold, and precious stones.
And when the queen of Sheba had seen all the wisdom of Solomon, the house that he had built, the food of his table, the seating of his officials, and the attendance of his servants, their clothing, his cupbearers, and his burnt offering which he offered at the house of the Lord, there was no more spirit in her.
And she said to the king, "The report was true which I heard in my own land of your affairs and of your wisdom, but I did not believe the reports until I came and my own eyes had seen it; and, behold, the half was not told me; your wisdom and prosperity surpass the report which I heard.

1 Kings 10:1–2, 4–7

And the time that Solomon reigned in Jerusalem over all Israel was forty years. And Solomon slept with his fathers, and was buried in the city of David his father; and Rehoboam his son reigned in his stead. *1 Kings 11:42–43*

Rehoboam went to Shechem, for all Israel had come to Shechem to make him king. And they said to Rehoboam, "Your father made our yoke heavy. Now therefore lighten the hard service of your father und his heavy yoke upon us, and we will serve you." But the king did not hearken to the people. And when all Israel saw that the king did not hearken to them, the people answered the king,
   "What portion have we in David?
   We have no inheritance in the son of Jesse.
   To your tents, O Israel!
   Look now to your own house, David."
So Israel departed to their tents. But Rehoboam reigned over the people of Israel who dwelt in the cities of Judah. So Israel has been in rebellion against the house of David to this day. *1 Kings 12:1, 3–4, 15–17, 19*

Preceding pages: Bay in the Gulf of Aqabah near Elath, from here the gold-bearing ships of Solomon embarked.
Clay tablet with the inscription "Gold from Ophir."
Left: Egyptian princess, clay relief. The queen of Sheba may have had a similar hairdo.

In the thirty-eighth year of Asa king of Judah, Ahab the son of Omri began to reign over Israel, and Ahab the son of Omri reigned over Israel in Samaria twenty-two years. And Ahab the son of Omri did evil in the sight of the Lord more than all that were before him. And as if it had been a light thing for him to walk in the sins of Jeroboam the son of Nebat, he took for wife Jezebel the daughter of Eth-baal king of the Sidonians, and went and served Baal, and worshiped him. He erected an altar for Baal in the house of Baal, which he built in Samaria. And Ahab made an Asherah. Ahab did more to provoke the Lord, the God of Israel, to anger than all the kings of Israel who were before him.
1 Kings 16: 29–33

Ben-hadad the king of Syria gathered all his army together; thirty-two kings were with him, and horses and chariots; and he went up and besieged Samaria, and fought against it. And the king of Israel went out, and captured the horses and chariots, and killed the Syrians with a great slaughter.
1 Kings 20: 1, 21

For three years Syria and Israel continued without war. So the king of Israel and Jehoshaphat the king of Judah went up to Ramoth-gilead.

But a certain man drew his bow at a venture, and struck the king of Israel between the scale armor and the breast-plate; therefore he said to the driver of his chariot, "Turn about, and carry me out of the battle, for I am wounded." And about sunset a cry went through the army, "Every man to his city, and every man to his country!"
So the king died, and was brought to Samaria; and they buried the king in Samaria. And they washed the chariot by the pool of Samaria, and the dogs licked up his blood, and the harlots washed themselves in it, according to the word of the Lord which he had spoken.
1 Kings 22: 1, 29, 34, 36–38

In those days the Lord began to cut off parts of Israel. In the twenty-third year of Joash the son of Ahaziah, king of Judah, Jehoahaz the son of Jehu began to reign over Israel in Samaria, and he reigned seventeen years. He did what was evil in the sight of the Lord, and followed the sins of Jeroboam the son of Nebat, which he made Israel to sin; he did not depart from them. And the anger of the Lord was kindled against Israel, and he gave them continually into the hand of Hazael king of Syria and into the hand of Ben-hadad the son of Hazael. *2 Kings 10: 32; 13: 1–3*

Right: King Ahab's wall in Samaria, the capital of Israel after its separation from the kingdom of Judah with its capital Jerusalem.
Following pages: Head of a Phoenician woman, ivory.
Bronze statuette of a Phoenician goddess of the kind worshiped by Israel in the northern kingdom.
Clay model of a chariot with two warriors.
Well in the Palace of Samaria, built in the reign of King Ahab. At such a pool dogs licked up the blood of the slain king as a sign of Yahweh's anger.

In the fourth year of King Hezekiah, which was the seventh year of Hoshea son of Elah, king of Israel, Shalmaneser king of Assyria came up against Samaria and besieged it and at the end of three years he took it.

In the fourteenth year of King Hezekiah Sennacherib king of Assyria came up against all the fortified cities of Judah and took them.

And the king of Assyria sent the Tartan, the Rabsaris, and the Rabshakeh with a great army from Lachish to King Hezekiah at Jerusalem. And they went up and came to Jerusalem. When they arrived, they came and stood by the conduit of the upper pool, which is on the highway to the Fuller's Field.

And that night the angel of the Lord went forth, and slew a hundred and eighty-five thousand in the camp of the Assyrians; and when men arose early in the morning, behold, these were all dead bodies.

2 Kings 18:9–10, 13, 17; 19:35

Zedekiah was twenty-one years old when he began to reign, and he reigned eleven years in Jerusalem. He did what was evil in the sight of the Lord his God. He did not humble himself before Jeremiah the prophet, who spoke from the mouth of the Lord. He also rebelled against King Nebuchadnezzar, who had made him swear by God.

Therefore the Lord brought up against them the king of the Chaldeans, who slew their young men with the sword in the house of their sanctuary, and had no compassion on young man or virgin, old man or aged; he gave them all into his hand. And all the vessels of the house of God, great and small, and the treasures of the house of the Lord, and the treasures of the king and of his princes, all these he brought to Babylon. And they burned the house of God, and broke down the wall of Jerusalem, and burned all its palaces with fire, and destroyed all its precious vessels. He took into exile in Babylon those who had escaped from the sword, and they became servants to him and to his sons until the establishment of the kingdom of Persia.

2 Chronicles 36:11–13, 17–20

By the waters of Babylon,
there we sat down and wept,
when we remembered Zion.
On the willows there
we hung up our lyres.
For there our captors
required of us songs,
and our tormentors, mirth, saying,
"Sing us one of the songs of Zion!"

How shall we sing the Lord's song
in a foreign land?
If I forget you, O Jerusalem,
let my right hand wither!
Let my tongue cleave to the roof of my mouth,
if I do not remember you,
if I do not set Jerusalem
above my highest joy!

Remember, O Lord, against the Edomites
the day of Jerusalem,
how they said, "Rase it, rase it!
Down to its foundations!"
O daughter of Babylon, you devastator!
Happy shall he be who requites you
with what you have done to us!
Happy shall he be who takes your little ones
and dashes them against the rock! *Psalm 137*

And the Lord says: "Because they have forsaken my law which I set before them, and have not obeyed my voice, or walked in accord with it, but have stubbornly followed their own hearts and have gone after the Baals, as their fathers taught them. Therefore thus says the Lord of hosts, the God of Israel: Behold, I will feed this people with wormwood, and give them poisonous water to drink. I will scatter them among the nations whom neither they nor their fathers have known; and I will send the sword after them, until I have consumed them."

"Behold, the days are coming, says the Lord, when I will raise up for David a righteous Branch, and he shall reign as king and deal wisely, and shall execute justice and righteousness in the land. In his days Judah will be saved, and Israel will dwell securely. And this is the name by which he will be called: 'The Lord is our righteousness.'

"Behold, the days are coming, says the Lord, when I will make a new covenant with the house of Israel and the house of Judah, not like the covenant which I made with their fathers when I took them by the hand to bring them out of the land of Egypt, my covenant which they broke, though I was their husband, says the Lord. But this is the covenant which I will make with the house of Israel after those days, says the Lord: I will put my law within them, and I will write it upon their hearts; and I will be their God, and they shall be my people. And no longer shall each man teach his neighbor and each his brother, saying, 'Know the Lord,' for they shall all know me, from the least of them to the greatest, says the Lord; for I will forgive their iniquity, and I will remember their sin no more."

Jeremiah 9:13–16; 23:5–6; 31:31–34

Comfort, comfort my people, says your God. Speak tenderly to Jerusalem, and cry to her that her warfare is ended, that her iniquity is pardoned, that she has received from the Lord's hand double for all her sins.

A voice cries: "In the wilderness prepare the way of the Lord, make straight in the desert a highway for our God. Every valley shall be lifted up, and every mountain and hill be made low; the uneven ground shall become level, and the rough places a plain. And the glory of the Lord shall be revealed, and all flesh shall see it together, for the mouth of the Lord has spoken."

Behold, the Lord God comes with might, and his arm rules for him; behold, his reward is with him, and his recompense before him. He will feed his flock like a shepherd, he will gather the lambs in his arms, he will carry them in his bosom, and gently lead those that are with young.

Who has measured the waters in the hollow of his hand and marked off the heavens with a span, enclosed the dust of the earth in a measure and weighed the mountains in scales and the hills in a balance?

Who has directed the Spirit of the Lord, or as his counselor has instructed him? Whom did he consult for his enlightenment, and who taught him the path of justice, and taught him knowledge, and showed him the way of understanding? Behold, the nations are like a drop from a bucket, and are accounted as the dust on the scales; behold, he takes up the isles like fine dust. Lebanon would not suffice for fuel, nor are its beasts enough for a burnt offering. All the nations are as nothing before him, they are accounted by him as less than nothing and emptiness. To whom then will you liken God, or what likeness compare with him?

But you, Israel, my servant, Jacob, whom I have chosen, the offspring of Abraham, my friend; fear not, for I am with you, be not dismayed, for I am your God; I will strengthen you, I will help you, I will uphold you with my victorious right hand. *Isaiah 40:1–5, 10–18; 41:8,10*

In the first year of Cyrus king of Persia, that the word of Lord by the mouth of Jeremiah might be accomplished, the Lord stirred up the spirit of Cyrus king of Persia so that he made a proclamation throughout all his kingdom and also put it in writing:

"Thus says Cyrus king of Persia: The Lord, the God of heaven, has given me all the kingdoms of the earth, and he has charged me to build him a house at Jerusalem, which is in Judah. Whoever is among you of all his people, may his God be with him, and let him go up to Jerusalem, which is in Judah, and rebuild the house of the Lord, the God of Israel – he is the God who is in Jerusalem."

Ezra 1: 1–3

The words of Nehemiah the son of Hacaliah. Now it happened in the month of Chislev, in the twentieth year, as I was in Susa the capital.

And the king said to me, "Why is your face sad, seeing you are not sick?" So I prayed to the God of heaven. And I said to the king, "If it pleases the king, and if your servant has found favour in your sight, that you send me to Judah, to the city of my fathers' sepulchres, that I may rebuild it."

So I came to Jerusalem and was there three days. I went out by night by the Valley Gate to the Jackal's Well and to the Dung Gate, and I inspected the walls of Jerusalem which were broken down and its gates which had been destroyed by fire. Then I went on to the Fountain Gate and to the King's Pool.

Then I said to the officials and the priests, "You see the trouble we are in, how Jerusalem lies in ruins with its gates burned. Come, let us build the wall of Jerusalem."

Nehemiah 1:1; 2:2, 4–5, 11, 13–14, 17

In the days of King Antiochus lawless men came forth from Israel, and misled many, saying, "Let us go and make a covenant with the Gentiles round about us, for since we separated from them many evils have come upon us." This proposal pleased them.

And the king sent letters by messengers to Jerusalem and the cities of Judah; he directed them to follow customs strange to the land, to forbid burnt offerings and sacrifices and drink offerings in the sanctuary, to profane sabbaths and feasts, to defile the sanctuary and the priests, to build altars and sacred precincts and shrines for idols, to sacrifice swine and unclean animals.

The Mattathias cried out in the city with a loud voice, saying: "Let every one who is zealous for the law and supports the covenant come out with me!"

1 Maccabees 1:44–47; 2:27

Right: Head of an Achaemenid king. Perhaps it represents Cyrus of Persia who allowed Israel to return to Jerusalem.
Following pages: Silver statuette of a Persian in traveling dress, of the period when Nehemia, in similar dress, traveled to Jerusalem.
The channel at the foot of the Ophel, which follows the course of the wall as rebuilt by Nehemia.
Greek dish showing the sacrifice of a pig, an unclean animal for Jews.
Coin from the time of the Maccabees showing the seven-branched candlestick of the Temple.